DEREK WALCOTT

THE HAITIAN TRILOGY

Derek Walcott was born in St. Lucia in 1930. His *Collected Poems: 1948–1984* was published in 1986; his subsequent works include the book-length poem *Omeros* (1990), *The Bounty* (1997), and, in an edition illustrated with his own paintings, *Tiepolo's Hound* (2000), all published by FSG. He received the Nobel Prize in Literature in 1992.

ALSO BY DEREK WALCOTT

POEMS

Selected Poems

The Gulf

Another Life

Sea Grapes

The Star-Apple Kingdom

The Fortunate Traveller

Midsummer

Collected Poems: 1948–1984

The Arkansas Testament

Omeros

The Bounty

Tiepolo's Hound

PLAYS

Dream on Monkey Mountain and Other Plays

The Joker of Seville and O Babylon!

Remembrance and Pantomime

Three Plays: The Last Carnival; Beef, No Chicken;
A Branch of the Blue Nile

The Odyssey

ESSAYS

What the Twilight Says

THE HAITIAN TRILOGY

HENRI CHRISTOPHE

DRUMS AND COLOURS

THE HAITIAN EARTH

THE HAITIAN TRILOGY

DEREK WALCOTT

FARRAR, STRAUS AND GIROUX

NEW YORK

Farrar, Straus and Giroux
19 Union Square West, New York 10003

Library of Congress Cataloging-in-Publication Data

Walcott, Derek.
  The Haitian trilogy / Derek Walcott.— 1st ed.
    p. cm.
  Contents: Henri Christophe—Drums and colours—The Haitian earth.
  ISBN 0-374-52813-6 (pbk. : alk. paper)
  1. Henri Christophe, king of Haiti, 1767–1820—Drama. 2. Haiti—
History—Revolution, 1791–1804—Drama. 3. Haiti—History—1804–1844—
Drama. 4. Haiti—Drama. I. Title.

PR9272.9.W3 H35 2001
812'.54—dc21

                                                          2001023158

Designed by Abby Kagan

www.fsgbooks.com

1   3   5   7   9   10   8   6   4   2

CONTENTS

FOREWORD

The writing of these plays spans an arc of nearly forty years. *Henri Christophe*, privately printed in 1948, deals with the struggle between two guerrilla generals, afterwards kings of Haiti, Christophe and Dessalines, following the imprisonment and death in exile of Toussaint L'Ouverture, whose name meant "the breach" or "the opening." It was written on the invitation of my brother, Roderick, and performed by a young group called the Arts Guild.

The theme of the slave revolt against French rule in Saint Domingue is also a pivotal part of the expansive design of *Drums and Colours*, commissioned for the first and only West Indian Federation, with emblematic images from Caribbean history: Columbus in chains, Millais's painting *The Boyhood of Raleigh*, the coachman of the Breda family Toussaint L'Ouverture, and the martyrdom of George William Gordon for Jamaican independence. *The Haitian Earth* includes a scene from *Drums and Colours*, a repetition seen in a slightly altered context.

The Haitian revolution, as sordidly tyrannical as so many of its subsequent regimes tragically became, was an upheaval, a necessary rejection of the debasements endured under a civilized empire, that achieved independence. The revolution is as central to the plays as it is to the history of the island.

My debt to all those involved in their production, many no longer here, to the Arts Guild of Saint Lucia, and to the Trinidad Theatre Workshop remains incalculable. This book is for the memory of my brother.

D.W.

2001

HENRI CHRISTOPHE

A Chronicle in Seven Scenes

The play was first produced by the St. Lucia Arts Guild at St. Joseph's Convent in Castries, St. Lucia, in 1949. Directed by Derek Walcott. Costumes by Alix Walcott.

It was later produced at Hans Crescent, London, in 1952. Directed by Errol Hill and designed by Carlyle Chang.

The cast was as follows:

GENERAL SYLLA—*Sam Morris*

GENERAL PÉTION—*Frank Pilgrim*

JEAN JACQUES DESSALINES—*Victor Patterson*

CORNEILLE BRELLE—*John Nunez*

HENRI CHRISTOPHE—*Errol John*

VASTEY—*Errol Hill*

NARRATOR—*George Lamming*

Also, MURDERERS, SOLDIERS, CROWD—*Roy Augier, Fred Debedin, Edric Roberts, George Griffith, Reggie Hill, Elesto Cortes, Ray Robinson, Maurice Mason, Eileen Stewart, Kenneth Monplaisir, Eustace Pollard, Lionel Ngakane, Charles Appia* (DRUMMER)

CAST OF CHARACTERS

GENERAL SYLLA

GENERAL PÉTION

JEAN JACQUES DESSALINES; *later Jacques I, King of Haiti*

CORNEILLE BRELLE, *a priest; afterwards archbishop*

HENRI CHRISTOPHE, *a general; later Henri I, King of
Haiti*

VASTEY, *his secretary; afterwards a baron*

NUMEROUS ATTENDANTS, GENERALS, MESSENGERS,
SOLDIERS, AND TWO MURDERERS

The setting is Haiti after 1803.

PART ONE

The cease of majesty

Dies not alone but like a gulf doth draw

What's near it with it; it is a massy wheel

Fix'd on the summit of the highest mount,

To whose huge spokes ten thousand lesser things

Are mortis'd and adjoin'd; which, when it falls,

Each small annexment, petty consequence,

Attends the boist'rous ruin.

—*Hamlet*

Scene 1

An interior of the Government Palace at Cap Haitien.
Present are GENERALS SYLLA *and* PÉTION. SYLLA *is an*
old, tired general with a wry, senile sense of humour. PÉTION
is active and middle-aged.

SYLLA

This waiting is exhausting. It's almost contradictory
That anything so sad can happen

7

In a broad afternoon.
Where's Dessalines?

PÉTION

Dressing in the inner room,
Preparing to be valedictory
To this peace that holds its breath, to hear
What happened to Toussaint.
Today a ship arrived from France;
Anchoring in the roads, she looked sullen;
Fearing the worst, Dessalines would look decorous
To suit the occasion. But if he really dressed his hope,
It would wear black; he would like Toussaint dead.
This country that stretched, crowing to greet
The sun of history rising, will have its throat cut;
That's the truth.

SYLLA

There's a kind of rustle in the lower hall;
It looks like the messenger from Napoleon, but
Where is Dessalines?

PÉTION

No doubt decorating his drawers
With epaulettes. He considers kingship;
Vanity will undo him.
Here's the messenger.

(*Enter* MESSENGER.)

What is the sum of the news, good or bad?

SYLLA

What is Napoleon doing?
Patience will drive us mad.

(*Enter* DESSALINES.)

This is the messenger from Napoleon
That we sent on the last ship; a veiled intensity
Inflates his bearing.

DESSALINES

Thanks. There is a crowd of marchands, fishermen
At the front gates. Are they converged in a rebellious
  murmur
For bread again, or waiting for news?

PÉTION

They want, as is only natural, to hear
About Toussaint.

DESSALINES

If they are rabble, make them orderly.
You smile, I do not.

PÉTION

About Toussaint . . . General . . .

DESSALINES

Of course, proceed. Be eloquent without elaboration;
Talk quickly . . .

MESSENGER

I have leave to speak?
After the general and liberator left his country,
By force and treachery of his ruined captains
He was taken, without satisfaction of audience or justice,
To a sullen castle, situated near the border,
Flung in a dungeon; he fretted there,
Complained of discomfort, protesting, not pleading,
As it suits a soldier, not a state buffoon.
But the black mountains and snow in the tight winter,
Whose sharpness, although cautionary in October,
Hurt his teeth, cramped in pains . . .

DESSALINES

Well? . . .

MESSENGER

He would look out past where the snow, like bread,
Settled without sound on the barred window edge
In brittle heaps. A mountain's iron aspect, the sky
Grey as soiled milk, imprisoned his exile more.
One day he rose to stretch his bones and died.
They buried him. The cleric who did the obsequies
Informed me that he died, grace on his lips;
But that is no comfort, he is dead . . .
You have heard his fate . . .

DESSALINES

I'll talk of fate. Have you letters
From Napoleon? How was his death received?

MESSENGER

Somewhat with courtesy, unlike the court
I see here. I expected to move iron men to tears;
You look as if I had discussed the weather.
Haiti is in the Saturday of honour, she
Is rudderless.

SYLLA

There are several captains, son.
Here is the priest. Thank you.
    (*Enter* BRELLE *as the* MESSENGER *leaves.*)
Good evening, *Père* Brelle.

BRELLE

I caught the mood from the tossing murmur outside;
I can read that the man is dead.
How they loved him . . .

DESSALINES

We have all loved him.
We must not profane his memory with idleness.
You have done well to come, Priest.
Have a proclamation issued; I'll append
My signature; declare a day of mourning, toll bells;
Inform your archbishop, Father Brelle, of an opulent
Obsequy for the man's memory. As for Christophe,
Tell him I have assumed temporary rule;
Temporary—see that the word is out before he chokes
The messenger. I am now in control.

Christophe must learn to cage the jaguar hope
In the bars of restraint. You all respect
My wish? . . . General Pétion? Sylla? Father Brelle?
Good. Tragedy threatens me with being great,
After this little condolence, the state . . .

BRELLE

This is a cursory mourning;
Do tears dry up so very quickly?

DESSALINES

Habit makes a boredom of tragedy.
Even in our eyes we hold death's annunciation,
Like Sylla, getting blind, deaths of twin light.
Let us proceed. We will enlarge our conscience, spread it
Like an open map in Father Brelle's presence.
There are no more French:
We have dispersed their broken units, they cannot lift a
    finger
Against us; the country, now, is ours;
But we must not talk, delay, malinger
With words, words, not action.

SYLLA

Then you appreciate the position
That a long war, an internal, cormorant war, has left
Our treasury in?
The peasants have identified liberty with idleness;

The fallow fields cropless; the old plantations,
Plaine du Nord, Morne Rouge, Quartier Morin,
Are like grass widows, unweeded, growing thorns
And bristles, dry seeds in a parching wind.
We do not seem to be able to drive them back to work;
They speak of slavery, murmur against measures,
Strict, but satisfactory to the able administrator.

PÉTION

Give a man an education or a gun
And you lose an honest labourer.

BRELLE

Since Toussaint's exile, I have observed the country
Has grown lax in spiritual matters, perplexing the clergy;
The ancient cults are growing like an unweeded garden over
Our pruned labours;
A stern but gentle hand is needed,
As long as the Church is not superseded.

SYLLA

We must remember Christophe;
He needs watching.

BRELLE

I do not descend to a question of enmity, I prefer
That the present holders of the keys of authority
Do not consider

Who must open the door first, rather,
Work in an amity to put our rooms in order.

PÉTION

I agree with what Brelle says;
We should transcend these partisan rages . . .

DESSALINES

Cackling of old women, talking politics to savages,
You still persist in framing gentle laws?
I have seen virgin debauchery, bacchanals, heresies, shouting
Under a swaying moon, drinking goat's death and wine,
A shriek ahead of spinsterish piety.
We should know better, not be merciful.
Iron decisions make a Caesar, and a Caesar is what
This country needs.
I will assemble powers.
I plan a temporary amendment, call it enlargement
Of Toussaint's constitution. If these men will not work,
Since we have their good in our intentions,
We will punish them like a stern father.

BRELLE

You will have to contend with the aristocracy.

SYLLA

What aristocracy? Treacherous white rags of flesh,
Dogs under skin, who sold his exile for the Judas kiss

Of comfort. Welcoming Toussaint when he routed Rigaud,
Throwing jewelry and laughter under his horse—
How many are left now? Not enough to spit on.

BRELLE

When will this eating another be over?

PÉTION

For you, that's easy; your cassock makes you calm;
But I remember in these soft-edged voices,
In the waning sun, actions so fresh
The gutters seem to run like lymph; the smell
Of blood cooks in my nostrils, the blood sticks
Wet, very wet, on my memory.

BRELLE

We cannot answer vengeance on vengeance, because
As far as the eye can warn, the incision instruct,
The cycle will never end. Blood grows
Where blood is uprooted . . .

SYLLA

Father, a priest, you are safe.
Dessalines is right, we'd better watch the whites.
I saw them fawn on Leclerc, your very archbishop,
Who owed to Toussaint his ecclesiastic spiral,
Leaped nimbly to the side that wore his flesh, the whites:
His robes did not hinder him.

BRELLE

You seek to kill the founders of your country?

DESSALINES

Who are the founders of our country—the Big Whites?
Wild geese that, adopting a finer climate, assume
The white divinity of the swan; and all their brothers,
A babble of shopkeepers, murderers, dispossessed.
You say they founded this country. What did they found?
Bastardhoods whose existences they denied, privileges
        pruned,
Cruelties devised to adorn an indolent minute,
White Jesuit fathers built presbyteries from slavery,
Swinging annulling incense over wound-humped backs,
Tired with the weight of Africa,
Baptising with a tongue in cheek . . .

SYLLA

Stop, Jacques, this ordinary heresy . . .

PÉTION

Shut up, old man.

BRELLE

I too have seen much; the actions of the Church
Are not always exemplary, but the Church's laws are perfect.
Messengers miscarry, fall prey to the time's temptation,
And the Church has done grave wrongs in Haiti,

Or where it has not done, it has often allowed it.

I grant Archbishop Mainvielle treacherous, refractory,

And I condemn him as a man, but

I cannot question his right to bless his flock . . .

DESSALINES

I have decided.

Although it defy an old archbishop whose voice

Is weak as water.

BRELLE

The archbishop is ineffectual. If

I were archbishop . . .

DESSALINES

When you will be archbishop, I will not be King,

And if I am King, you will never be archbishop. So even
    priests

Conceal ambitions?

PÉTION

You seek to exclude and deprive the whites?

DESSALINES

Be frank, I seek to cut them down.

BRELLE

Massacre would be more frank.

DESSALINES

Call it any name, the syllables do not matter.

BRELLE

Whose conscience do you ferret out on that?
Whose law? What love?

DESSALINES

My own, my conscience, and the memory
Of a red past.

BRELLE

Conscience is the jackass you ride to history on, the mule
You heap excuses on, but watch your step.
You defame Toussaint.
What is your alphabet, the bullet?
What is the bayonet, your bible?
You betrayed Toussaint to Leclerc,
Then you betrayed the peasants to Rochambeau.
What is your dictionary, only treason?
Then, when the tide changed, you betrayed the French.
If I had the authority . . .

DESSALINES

Priest, your cassock is your comfort; do not waste
Your safety, leave us.

BRELLE

So you must rule?
I hope Christophe contests it.

You throne yourself on cruelty. So you will rule?
We are embarrassment to our hopes, when
They are fulfilled. Ah, time, how men shame
The achievement of their whispers!
You are bald of mercy. But I warn all of you,
The extreme of tyranny happens when
The gaoled turn on their gaolers.
I've said my fill.

(*He exits.*)

DESSALINES

And overflowed the cup.
Now, gentlemen, to make our policy plain,
Our simple trick impedes Christophe:
The messenger hastens cautiously to his camp,
Days later will arrive too late.
Christophe will be helpless to prison power.
I assume a monarchy.

(*There is consternation.*)

PÉTION

Monarchy . . . Not even Toussaint . . .

SYLLA

Christophe will work a civil war against it.

DESSALINES

Who is Christophe? My victory over Rochambeau
Here at Cap Haitien rides freshly on my crest.

We have beaten the French, splintered
Napoleon's indestructibles, fever has furrowed them,
Sickness scythed them in harvest . . .
Think, gentlemen, a black nobility, the white flower
    destroyed.
But keep this in the antechambers of your secrecy.
Crack Christophe's spirit in open policy,
Force painful petitions from peasant mouths,
Force favour from fools, to make me King
Christophe cannot query petitions.
Publish a monarchy in your quiet hope.

SYLLA

We have spent the night making ourselves miserable
With riches; there is no hope in the grey dawn spreading
On a halcyon sea where dreams shrivel.

DESSALINES

What dreams? What dreams, old man?

SYLLA

They reassemble after Angelus;
When the drums beat a skull of death, they rustle sheets,
And utter blood to the moon—that same sharp moon
That is a scythe to clouds—clawing the sky.
I have had all these dreams in my sleeping tent.
We have all been great generals, but idleness
Is settling on us like a grave disease,

While Time is turning us from prowess to politics,
And age, advancing his last insignia, plants white-haired
    surrender,
Raises citadels of fatigue over the rubble;
Time has white hairs.
My eyes are sick, and I have dreams in this waste
After long war.
This is a silence that is more deadly
Than the silence smoking over the burnt city,
The dead corruption hanging over toothless walls, the heavy
Heat in air, over the burnt city;
We have no activity, only
Corrupted purposes.

PÉTION

These, at least, are old soldier's dreams,
Easily explained.
We must dress for the early Memorial Mass.

SYLLA

I wonder how the dawn breaks
For Christophe; what comfort does it afford
His soldier's repose?

DESSALINES

For an old man, you certainly talk
A lot of bloody rubbish.
I shall have coffee served, and then to church,

To pray for Toussaint grinning among
Pink idle angels . . .

PÉTION

Yes, Your Majesty.

(DESSALINES *looks at him cautiously, then smiles, then
bursts into laughter, as the bell sounds and the lights fade out.*)

Scene 2

CHRISTOPHE'*s camp at Les Cayes. Dusk. The sonorous
tolling of the cathedral bell in the preceding scene is imitated
by the sound of a ship's bell in the distance. Three* SOLDIERS
*are facing the gentle suspiration of an open tent, quietly, as
though expecting someone to emerge. A flag with an
escutcheon streams on the strong sea wind.*

FIRST SOLDIER

The news is good, I feel it in my bones.

SECOND SOLDIER

These messengers are too circumspect; they
Could have told the officers.

THIRD SOLDIER

I wonder what has become of Toussaint.

FIRST SOLDIER

I cannot wait to hear what I fear and expect,
That if Toussaint is dead, we have lost our respect.
We stand like gargoyles in the Angelus
That speaks a cruelty we cannot endure, and the ship's bell
Clappers a lost creed to a ruined army.
I seem to see, now that the sky bleeds, spreading
The sea with a luxurious death, I think I see
Hope falling like the sun from the empty air.

SECOND SOLDIER

Toussaint is dead.
If he were living, Christophe would have said.

FIRST SOLDIER

We talk nonsense.
Dessalines has sent the last standards scattering
North at Le Cap, flung their strength from the last
    promontory,
Split their authority over the narrow sea.
Napoleon is numb, although he has Toussaint.
If Toussaint returns, and that is impossible . . .
Dessalines meditating monarchy in the burnt city,
And Christophe here, far from a corrupt city,
Thinks of the day his sun alone shall hang
In the sky's arena, without
Dessalines's interference.

THIRD SOLDIER

I cannot imagine Toussaint dead.
Here is the general.

CHRISTOPHE (*Coming from his tent.*)
Why are the men here?

THIRD SOLDIER

For news, any news, General;
We saw the ship anchor hours ago,
Saw you hold conference with heaviness;
Curiosity and love laid us close;
We wait here, hoping.

CHRISTOPHE

Fold up your hopes to show them to your children,
Because the sun has settled now
Behind the horizon of our bold history.
Now no man can measure the horizon
Of his agony; this grief is wide, wide,
A ragged futility that beats against these rocks, like
Sea-bell's Angelus.
The man is dead, history has betrayed us . . .

FIRST SOLDIER

You talk of duplicity; you yourself betrayed him.
I think we mock-turtle him with tears.

CHRISTOPHE

These sharp tears that prick my heart are genuine,
And as for betrayal, who has not betrayed?
Mainvielle the archbishop, Ogé, Dessalines, Telemaque,
And I, time, I.
Toussaint . . .
I cannot list his braveries, I can only tell
Things that the memory shudders to remember,
Hurt by its love. He broke three nations,
He disrupted intrigues, curbed civil wars;
He was no hammock general directing fools
Into a cannon's yawn, he rode to wars with you,
He held his generals, although they were refractory,
Like those who triumphed in Troy after
The duplicity of the horse—
Sylla, Maurepas, Dessalines, Pétion;
He forded rivers, a furious forager.
But now, they tell me, he, made limp in spirit,
Crucified in a winter's stubborn nails,
An old man dancing on a stick of time, all skin and groan,
Wearing respectability to rags, died,
Coughing on a stone floor.
All this because a man was black.
But we must triumph. Under that winter death
I will perform the rites of spring, if
You will let me, or let Dessalines . . .
We need more than a wavering sceptre in this twilight.
Slavery must never hold us again, not while
I live.

(*They cheer.*)

Call in the chaplain, or the priest at Les Cayes, let
The quartermaster distribute no more liquor, call
Mourning through the regiment, and tell the chaplain,
Conduct a Mass under the mourning trees.
Make sorrow severe as it suits a soldier.
I want to see my captains. To your offices.
Today we break camp for Cap Haitien. Where
Are my lieutenants?

(*The* SOLDIERS *leave.* VASTEY *and another* GENERAL *who
have emerged quietly during* CHRISTOPHE*'s elegy remain
behind. With the* SOLDIERS *gone,* CHRISTOPHE*'s whole
bearing changes immediately.*)

Why was I not informed earlier?
Here there is only talk of intrigues, policies,
While Dessalines rules. Caution and discussion
Are fatal. We have slipped the chance to hold time by the
   tail,
Bystanders at our own loss.

GENERAL

Has this affected us so much?

VASTEY

Dessalines is dangerous. Restless rulers
Dream to their pillows of personal power.
Now that Toussaint's dead, the choice is open
To the strong man.

CHRISTOPHE

Do you advocate rebellion
Against the republic?

VASTEY

No, General, you misunderstand. I do not consider
Dessalines democratic as, say, Toussaint taught:
He nurses whispers, imperial ambitions;
He will work without council, and oppress the poor.

GENERAL

He will want to be King. Toussaint
Never assumed this.

CHRISTOPHE

History has duped me; I, who was a leader,
Shall now play school to a pawn, a breeder
Of petty hates in which I am part.
Pétion is an actor, he too is no pawn.
If we could assemble and wait . . .

GENERAL

What does the general decide, after all:
Will he wrench the fruit green from the stalk,
Or will he wait for it to rot, and fall?

VASTEY

My personal advice is: In your talk,
Do not be too smooth, show your discontent

At being brushed off the chessboard of history;
But play the pieces on the board with duplicity,
Until you are King by the hand of history.

CHRISTOPHE

You are fools; I do not tie the shoelaces of history;
I am the history of which you speak.

VASTEY

Yet I know our army to be far from weak;
Civil war, I think, should crown us in a week.

CHRISTOPHE

But the country is much too paupered by malevolences,
Conquests, fevers, ruins, to stand a war of brother against
    brother.
We must try other ways, other chances.
So this is the waste country I inherit,
A stepping-stone to former slaves . . .

GENERAL

Were we not all slaves, General?

CHRISTOPHE

A king flows in me.
You have seen me command,
Cruel and kingly when I burned Le Cap,
Rochambeau realmless, harried to France.

I judge my conduct
In a king's eyes and find this failure.

VASTEY

The riot we expected is routed. Why idle here?
You love your country; but that should not disfigure
Self-love out of proportion.
Pétion is placed as awkwardly as we are.
I would advise a secret exchange of views
On the possibilities of a joint control.

CHRISTOPHE

I understand your philosophy, put the self first.
No, gentlemen, the soldiers are sick of savagery;
We will sit outside the chambers of their policy.
When Dessalines is deposed
By his own despair,
We shall wear popularity openly like the sun.
Command the removal of this regiment to the north;
We'll see what Dessalines is worth.
I'm for some sleep inside.
. . . Good night.

(*He exits.*)

GENERAL

Christophe is a two-sided mirror; under
His easy surface, ripples of dark
Strive with the light, or like a coin's two sides,

Or like the world half-blind when moons are absent,
And brilliant in the glare of sun.
Under that certain majesty he hides
The teaching of Toussaint, the danger of Dessalines.

VASTEY

I am tired of war; I want a little money.
But I'd make war to get money.
Christophe loves Haiti, like himself, cruelly.
But like a well-intentioned physician, he bleeds
It too much.
But we had better sleep before the march;
Tomorrow, three days late, we will ride under an arch
Garlanded with plots, festooned with cruelty and screens
Of treachery, hear people shouting,
"Long live Dessalines . . ."
Does that frighten you, m'sieur?

(*They exit. The* GENERAL *lingers, thinking, then goes out slowly, as the lights fade.*)

Scene 3

The conference room, or the same as Scene 1. VASTEY *taking dictation laboriously from* CHRISTOPHE *at a desk. Through a middle curtain half-opened, the throne can be seen, patient and empty. From time to time,* CHRISTOPHE *casts glances at it.*

CHRISTOPHE

". . . all applications to be forwarded to the office of the
Commissioner of Internal Affairs, Cap Haitien. By order,
Henri Christophe. For Jacques le Premier." Good, Vastey?
I have noticed the present conduct of this King;
He rules with a drunkard hand, heavily,
Knowing only a government by guile.
Have you seen the estates, Vastey?
    (VASTEY *proffers the document, which he signs awkwardly.*)
The grass overruns the aristocratic urns,
The weeds grow between broken coachwheels
That the wind spins in an empty season, the rich ruined.
Toussaint would have liked that: but no flowering
Peace, only poverty, a souring
Idle crop, an overpowering
Stench of tyranny.

VASTEY

Yes, sir. This copy . . .

(CHRISTOPHE *waves it aside vaguely.*)

CHRISTOPHE

Do you mock me?
            (*He says this indulgently.*)
You know I cannot read.
Reread them, are they intact?
I hope you have not obscured plain fact
In a smoke of Latin expressions?

VASTEY

There are no digressions.

Shall I read it to you, sir?

CHRISTOPHE

Oh Lord, no.

(*He sits down.*)

Today, another meeting. I am ashamed, recalling
　　councils

Of war, before Pierrot, and when we splintered

Them at Ennery, now up to my neck

In paper, a tired commissioner.

I think that if I went to war again,

I would bleed ink, so many papers, white men's ways.

Where are the others?

Get the notes for my report.

Locked in these laces, captive in silk . . .

Colourless courtesan of a rival ruler,

Old dog with no teeth . . .

VASTEY

The King, look at the throne, is

Out again killing offenders,

Washing his pity in blood.

Will he be here?

CHRISTOPHE

Don't know. Go for the notes.

VASTEY

Here come the others, but
No King.

(*He exits.*)

CHRISTOPHE

Come in, gentlemen, the King
Will come.

(*Enter* SYLLA, PÉTION, *and a* GENERAL.)

Good evening, gentlemen, sit down.
How are you, m'sieu, m'sieu, and you, General Pétion?
What are you smiling at, General?

PÉTION

Your new role, Henri; you wear it so mildly
It breeds suspicions. You must not preside
With such superior sarcasm.

(*General laughter as they sit.*)

CHRISTOPHE (*Wryly amused*)

I have sent my secretary for a statement
Concerning the finances; you have observed the state
Of the country? The old plantations
Stand haggard as prisoners, the windmills have broken
    arms,
The soldiers not sent home, murmurs mounting,
While the King wastes money like blood,
Slaughtering his "enemies."

SYLLA

Who are our enemies?

Not complexions, heresies, but time;

The gusts of years, the . . .

(*He says this almost privately, but they listen.*)

CHRISTOPHE

I am his enemy, if he continues.

Do not interrupt, old man;

Kings rule and grow corrupt,

Absolute authority can only disrupt

The church and state. Murmurs erupt

To anarchy, the peasants will kill.

PÉTION

You talk like Brelle.

Have you gone to church lately?

(*Laughter.*)

CHRISTOPHE

You are a mulatto, you must hate me

For this insolent love.

I am only a soldier, a poor fish; you are all whales

Thrashing about in political machinations.

I have done as the constitution has demanded,

My men dismissed, my power disbanded.

SYLLA

Not disbanded, but cut down.

Are you not safe? The French are far,

The treasury is without the wherewithal

To equip soldiers who should be on plantations,

The war is long over.

You have been identified as your country's lover.

Discard the despair of ceaseless argument;

If the farmers dispute the open property,

The land will fester under those who love her,

The plough hidden in the tall grasses, ruin, the cabin

Remain with unhinged doors, the children

Play in the pools of blood in front of the door.

Where is this peace that the French used to mock?

We pull a rock

On our heads, if we starve a tired people.

CHRISTOPHE

You should have chosen the soapbox

Or the steeple. Thank you.

(*He notices* VASTEY.)

Come. Vastey, help me distribute testaments

Of our poverty. Read these, gentlemen,

And observe our industry.

(*He distributes papers, which provoke a mild consternation,*
which petrifies as soon as he says . . .)

His Majesty, the King of Haiti.

(*They rise. The whole gesture is one of mock solemnity that irritates* DESSALINES.)

DESSALINES

Thank you, Henri. Sit down.
  (*He himself is about to sit when* CHRISTOPHE *ironically indicates the throne and* VASTEY *parts the curtain.*
    DESSALINES *hesitates, suffering the little joke.*)
Thanks. Well, be quick.
              (*He sits on the throne.*)
What is it you want, Commissioner?

CHRISTOPHE

Patience, Yo . . . Jean . . . I mean Your Majesty.

(*Laughter.*)

DESSALINES

You are rude, Henri, I am a king, no political toy.

CHRISTOPHE

And I was a general before I was a schoolboy.

PÉTION

Please, please.

DESSALINES

You envy me, you wear a hurt pride.

CHRISTOPHE

I consider the articles expressed
In your constitution, and I find,
Hidden in your assembly's salad of words, dressed
In a kind of poison to any freedom,
An evidence of autocracy.
You have decided to assume a monarchy
Before Toussaint's breath faded from the glass of history;
You consulted a clique only, a class
With twisted personal interests at its mind's end.
In this rule there is an end
Of democracy, only a long exploitation
And a bitter harvest, an expiration
Of the breath of decency, financial depression;
And I was never asked to give my impression.

DESSALINES

You see what it amounts to, gentlemen; Christophe's
    advice
On a subject we all have agreed on twice;
Consider the popular petition:
I rule because of the people's decision.

CHRISTOPHE

Nonsense, rubbish.

(*They are all shocked to an electric silence.*)

DESSALINES

I am the King! Henri, never
Forget that. Sit back in your places.

CHRISTOPHE

Then rule like one,
With a king's grace, not a king's grimaces,
You keep your own people in virtual slavery.

DESSALINES

I am the King. Your present bravery
Goes well on my battlefields, not in my chambers.

CHRISTOPHE

Haiti must suffer from those who hate her.

DESSALINES

Mind you do not go too far.
So I hate Haiti? I wish you were King.

CHRISTOPHE

That is not my wish.

DESSALINES

Every slave dreams in extremes,
And we were both, Henri.
You think I am tricking you? I am your friend.

CHRISTOPHE

I am the friend of the people.

We must avoid opportunities of separation;
You kill offenders because of their complexion;
Where is the ultimate direction of this nation,
An abattoir of war?

DESSALINES

I who was a slave am now a king,
And being a king, remember I was slave;
What shall I live as now, a slave or king?
Being this King chains me to public breath
Worse than chains. I cannot have a masque
Before some slave scoops up a gutter tale
To fling into my face; I cannot drink
Red wine unless the linen rustles blood; I cannot break bread
Before an archbishop canonizes a body
Broken, stuck like an albatross on the hill of skulls.
Well, I will not listen.
White men are here; for every scar
                    (*He bares his tunic.*)
Raw on my unforgiving stomach, I'll murder children,
I'll riot. I have not grown lunatic, I'll do it, I'll do it.
You think I am not aware of your intrigues,
Mulattos and whites, Brelle and Pétion;
I am a king: Argue with history.
Ask history and the white cruelties
Who broke Boukmann, Ogé, Chavannes; ask Rochambeau.
If you will not comply, I'll go.

(*He exits.*)

CHRISTOPHE

That is the crazy graph of power,
The zenith of his climb; he thinks himself colossus, but size
Spells ruin, the earth is cracking now under his girth.
We must look after us, or he will . . .
A lunatic king.

SYLLA

If I could only warn, a grey-haired harbinger,
Helpless as time to warn her pupils;
There is nothing more to life, gentlemen,
Than to find a positive function for the money in the blood
To culture peace.
The meeting is over,
Nothing gained again. Good night. Brelle
Will be amused and terrified.

(*Exit all but* CHRISTOPHE *and* PÉTION.)

CHRISTOPHE

Sylla hangs to the archbishop
Like an innocent child; with wagging tongue
Around a father's knee, preparing for death
By logic and loves.

PÉTION

What is it you want, Henri?

(CHRISTOPHE *closes the door.*)

CHRISTOPHE

Sit down.

PÉTION

Yes?

CHRISTOPHE

I think it is boredom that has put him so;
Blood grows into a habit with a born butcher;
He has grown into something monstrous
From thirteen years of war . . .

PÉTION

I am not as gentle as he thinks;
War has begun to crease my face with savagery;
It is worn like an old cavalry boot;
But if he thinks a king's authority
Beggars morality, he had better reject priests.

CHRISTOPHE

However, he has never sought to harm the clergy;
Although he does not find much favour with the archbishop,
He has never killed a priest.

PÉTION

To think that for two days now he has been
Martyring children with a tired sword! He is a model

Of horror. Dessalines is only a beast;
He goes to blood with the joy that I go to a feast.
There must be some revision
Of his absurd and useless decision.

CHRISTOPHE (*Slyly*)
You are thinking of treason and anarchy.
Has he not good reason to adopt a monarchy?

PÉTION
Because he fought to protect his country
Does he think he has bought its soul and its duty?
For my part I do not care who rules,
As long as he loves his country and rules
Well. But he commands a tyranny of fools,
Who spell wounds, not words, their sabres their schools;
I will not be one and stain
The memory of Toussaint's intention;
I will resist tyranny on pain of expulsion.

CHRISTOPHE
His last deeds fill me to the brim with revulsion.
He is not fit to rule, but on revision,
I find that our patriotism leaps the boundary
Of duty, and this is our quandary:
Whether our duty is to country or King;
This is the problem, between the spirit
Of love and the material duty: that is the thing.

PÉTION

His death is for his country's merit.

CHRISTOPHE

And when he is dead, who shall inherit?
You of course are more fit.

PÉTION

That is a matter solved after the riddle;
You want to begin somewhere in the middle.
As for myself, I halt at assuming
A blood-whispering cloak, gripping the sceptre he gripped,
Squatting on the throne from which he slipped.
Besides, you are better equipped.
I am a mulatto, the Negroes are in the majority,
Present rule is only your authority.
Or, after he is dead, with a twin constituency
We could contest rule.

CHRISTOPHE

You mean one of us King?

PÉTION

I was thinking
Rather in terms of a presidency.

CHRISTOPHE

You would have the public vote.

PÉTION

I'm sure I would not.
Mon Dieu, look how time has made us politicians
Rather than soldiers!

CHRISTOPHE

So I must kill my friend. How will we do it?
On a matter of a massacre, I'm one of the expert
    technicians.
But to kill a friend . . .

PÉTION

That is only the only means to an end.

CHRISTOPHE

It is true that the country is ruined.
And the French may return. It will have to be done
Secretly, not in an open rebellion.
One of my soldiers . . . Pétion, you must go south
To avoid suspicion; please do not mistake my purpose.
Besides, he swears that he will deal with the mulattos
After he slaughters the whites;
Wait at Les Cayes, or stay near Port-au-Prince;
I will arm your forces to seize the sceptre from him.
Meanwhile, I will remain here and hide the snake
In my pawn's fawning; he still considers me.
Mass power in the South; I will weaken
Him by duplicity. I think the time is ripe:
The fruit is going to be wrenched from the stalk.

PÉTION

And the other generals, Sylla, Paul Prompt, Blondin—can
They be trusted to a man?

CHRISTOPHE

Each of them thinks nightly of being a king.
It is a peasant's vanities.
We will tell them nothing.

PÉTION

And if they know . . .

CHRISTOPHE

To know is nothing; to hinder is execution.

PÉTION

You are firm in your dreams as in your solution.

CHRISTOPHE

What do you know of my dreams?

PÉTION

Nothing except that by hiding them you admit
Their existence. Excuse me. I must go south.
God help us in our purposes as in our ambitions.

CHRISTOPHE

God help our ambitions to the gates of our purposes.
(PÉTION *shakes his hand and leaves.*)

I must do it.

(*A knock.*)

Who is it?

Come in.

(*A* MESSENGER *enters.*)

Speak, soldier, why are you so dirty?

MESSENGER

I am all out of breath, General.

CHRISTOPHE

Not general, commissioner. Next time gather,

Please, your breath in the yard, rather

Than enter scared to death.

MESSENGER

The King sent me in anger.

He says that now there is no more danger.

CHRISTOPHE

Give me the message in the rough.

MESSENGER

Well, sir,

The soldiers, idle in their narrow barracks,

Tired already of thirteen years of war,

Had planned a liberation from their captains.

Next day the Emperor came riding through the ranks,

Waving a sword that sparkled in the sun,

Commanding all his blacks to slaughter whites.
And there were some of us who, tasting blood,
Hearing this trumpet summon like a wound,
Felt the old call: we leapt into his arms,
And held our smoking rifles by the paws;
He held us burning through the sleeping streets,
Meeting a herd of idlers, who raggedly conjured
A vomit from the horn of plenty.
Two hours we raged the city, raping, rioting,
Turning with slaughter the chapels into brothels.
I skewered a white martyr under an altar,
We flung one girl in an uncertain arc
Into the bloody bosom of the pier, and over us
This King rode, looking as though he chewed his
    corpses,
His eyes all arson. And now that massacre
Tires him, he comes home to his bed,
To tell the generals that Haiti,
Thank him, is safe,
From prejudice, from pain.

CHRISTOPHE

You have done your duty, I must do mine.
            (*The* MESSENGER *exits.*)
I cannot kill my friend.
But this King is not my friend; our ambitions rub,
They want to sit on an only throne.

(*Enter* DESSALINES, *dishevelled, sword in his hand.*)

DESSALINES

Henri, my friend, you look ill.

CHRISTOPHE

I am not as ruddy as you.

DESSALINES

You mock my colour.
You cannot think a black king real.

CHRISTOPHE

I am black, too, but today I am ashamed.
You have red work on your hands.

DESSALINES

It was a necessary horror,
A crop of murders, necessary
Like death. I know it will not let me sleep from now.

CHRISTOPHE

You have no soul, no thought
Of paying afterwards?

DESSALINES

No, Henri, this is politics.
I cannot wear, Christ-like, an albatross
Around my neck; the wounds in my sides
Were dug by innocent white hands; a king
Makes them pay for it.

CHRISTOPHE

No twinge of soul?

DESSALINES

I act like a king; a king is whole;
A king's wrongs are a king's privileges.

CHRISTOPHE

You wound and use authority for bandages.
You are sick, a peevish king with terrible whims.
Sit down, you are tired.
Scarcely an hour ago, it seems,
I was plotting with Pétion to assassinate you,
But I know now I cannot hate you.
I will admit our treason,
But it is past now, and your condition is the reason:
You are sick. We planned Pétion's going south,
Rebellion against you with me in the north,
But no more. What is it, Jacques? . . .

DESSALINES

I carved a passage, rigorous as a dolphin
Through the red fun. Oh, three wars cannot size
Yesterday's horror.
And yet I had no purpose for this fighting.
Have I gone mad, after long war?
Does murder grow like habit in the hand, infection
In the fingers and the skull?
Henri, I am mad . . .

CHRISTOPHE

Something will be done.

DESSALINES

Yes . . .

CHRISTOPHE

For your own good.
But we must watch Pétion. Tomorrow you ride south
To stall the insurrection.
Tonight I will see the light in your
Room is put out.

DESSALINES

You are my friend, you understand
What I need most.

CHRISTOPHE (*Dimly*)

Yes. Yes. Yes.

(*Slow fade-out.*)

Scene 4

A wood at twilight, outside the city. Two MURDERERS
onstage, arguing.

FIRST MURDERER

What you want to think about it for? Hold the knife so.
Then get somewhere soft and mortal, put the blade in, and

think you cutting meat, and don't bother your head about religion. What wrong in that? . . .

SECOND MURDERER

It's only I am not 'custom . . .

FIRST MURDERER

You don't want to become a professional?

SECOND MURDERER

Yes, sir . . . but . . .

FIRST MURDERER

Well, you shaming your father. I remember how he was always saying you would make such a good apprentice. What is the matter, you are scared of a little blood? You never kill a crab, or a chicken, or an old woman? You all are funny, yes! You kill a man who was an evil king, marry him to the tall dust he grew from; you kill him intelligently, cleanly, no disfiguration; you give him time to pray, and if he does not want, you can say it for him after, just a few *Ave Maria*s, and the act of contrition, and then you know you can leave that grey King slain under the red trees and know you do a good job. You don't even have to worry 'bout the grass growing out of his sockets, the dead leaves rusting for days over his quiet lips, and the tall grass lecturing in whispers about what good all this thing is for . . . But then you think that after you kill him everything done? You think people glad for it? Listen . . .

(*He goes into an elaborate pantomime.*)

Finish? No, it isn't. "Soldiers, ladies and gentlemen! A murder has been done, murder, ladies, murder, gentlemen, against the law of gods. Murder? We must—quiet, ladies, quiet, gentlemen—we must apprehend the killer. Apprehend him." And then you run, your mouth open, your eyes streaming, with hounds and humans in an inhuman comedy chasing you to sanctuary . . . Sanctuary? What, in an abbey where they eat chicken, in a stable where they shoot horses, in gaol where they break your neck?

(*He grows quiet, impressing the young man.*)

And then they take you to treat you to the same argument they use against you. Thou shalt not kill. God has given no man right to kill, tell that to the lawyer, and the gaoler, and the warder, and particularly to the rope that cannot understand logic and argument. What will the priest say . . . "My boy, it was murder that hung Christ like an albatross around the neck of Golgotha; my boy, you must not kill; take him away and God have mercy on his soul . . ." This place is an arena, a human arena of lions and laughter; only the wicked and those who do not think can survive. What are you laughing at?

SECOND MURDERER

Sorry, sir. Now, sir, what would you say are the best hints to become a professional murderer?

FIRST MURDERER

First, be a vegetarian; second, be kind to animals; third, keep in practice. Now you see this King, this Dessalines, watch me handle him. Now you must plan, and I will have already planned. Let us see what will happen. All right . . .

(*He sketches the campaign on the ground.*)

Look. The King is coming, we are here. He is with his calvary and going to Port-au-Prince. The soldiers throw him from his horse; they must not touch him, that is our job; they take his sword, he wanders off the road, while the dark settles, and here by the road we are going to wait, sharp and clean . . .

(*He raises his head, listening.*)

I hear horses. We can take his finery. You ever see an easier job? What is the matter with you? Where is your instrument? You mean you came here without an instrument? Boy, you are a shame to your father . . .

SECOND MURDERER (*In a frightened whisper*)

You not scared about . . . God or death?

(*Sound of horses, distantly, and voices.*)

We should not kill. Is that what my father used to do? We ca—

FIRST MURDERER

Keep quiet . . . keep quiet, boy, we must not think . . .

SECOND MURDERER

But to kill a man . . .

FIRST MURDERER

Ask the generals of the wars that are supposed to buy liberty and peace; ask them why they use ordinary people, workmen, niggers, and smiling boys with sonnets in their eyes dying like Greece on vulgar cannons; ask the man who hired us. I am his hand, he is his conscience.

SECOND MURDERER

And what about God?

FIRST MURDERER

Ask God why He killed His son, and what good it did us since . . .

SECOND MURDERER

You are a heretic and a murderer . . . He is coming . . .

(FIRST MURDERER *crouches, waiting; the other stands dazed, watching an opening in the bushes; the older man pulls him and strikes him silent.*)

FIRST MURDERER

Poor boy, yet what he says . . .
I have no authority to cut the throat of light,
I am tired of washing the blood from my hands, but
Who can pardon the hawk its instincts, the gull
Its flight from the storm, the vulture on the corpses that stink?
Who will pardon the hunter, not the friend, dead between
   three
Trees?

(DESSALINES *enters, dishevelled.*)

DESSALINES

Who are you?

(*Then he realizes.*)

Of course, so ordinary and professional . . .

No . . . please, please . . .

(*He is not in panic but trying to talk sense.*)

Listen . . .

(*Meanwhile, the* SECOND MURDERER, *on his knees, watches with fascination the horror that is about to be enacted.*)

FIRST MURDERER

Sir, let's be quiet about this . . .

(*He advances calmly and draws a knife with terrible leisure. The* SECOND MURDERER *buries his face in his hands and begins to mumble a kind of prayer, hardly audible, as the lights fade out.*)

PART TWO

The first that there did greet my stranger soul,
Was my great father-in-law, renowned Warwick;
Who cried aloud "What scourge for perjury
Can this dark monarchy afford false Clarence?"
—*Richard III*

Scene 1

Before the cathedral at Cap Haitien. SYLLA, VASTEY, *other*
GENERALS, *and* BRELLE *are on the cathedral steps. The
mitre of the archbishop makes the apex for the triangular
arrangement of the scene; on either side of the steps a* CROWD
is lined, all facing offstage.

SYLLA

This paupered love in the lazaretto
Of my grey-haired heart had anticipated
Peace and penance when we cracked them at Crête-à-Pierrot
When history sucked the last sail out of vision;
Now impossible, it seems, with

Jealousies snarling, greed
Plotting, with Pétion fighting Christophe:
Look now, a civil war.

BRELLE

What had you thought of?

SYLLA

I had hoped for, first, faith,
People singing, eating leisurely
Under the green ease of councils, a federation
Of complexions; but Haiti will never be normal;
Not I either, dying blind,
Will see it.

BRELLE

I see, Henri would prefer us to think
This fight for the presidency against Pétion
Necessary for us to get on;
But no poison is a necessary drink.
But Monsieur Vastey must think differently.

VASTEY

Of course, ingratitude.
Who would be President on Pétion's terms?
He had framed the Senate to a stronger constitution;
The President would have been the figurehead of an institution
He could not control, no more than I can halt storms.
The Senate was the body; he could not be the mouthpiece

Of factious members of a corrupted office;
If he had done nothing, he would be straw to their weathers,
A feather blown by their inclinations.

SYLLA

Well recited, schoolboy.

BRELLE

Well, why did he not present the cabinet their protestations?
Why settle by war what quarrels would?

VASTEY

The general believes the price of freedom is blood.

SYLLA

No one is more generous than generals;
I, one once, know that;
War is cheap.

VASTEY

How can you live with enemies around you,
Betrayal on the tongues of those who surround you
Ready to play cat and mouse?
Must Christophe not strengthen the floors of his house,
Before the whole collapse in dust?

SYLLA

While industry and the plough rust?
And the people murmur against this slaughter?

Was it not merely to appease an affront
That Christophe takes blood for an expense account:
"Tell Pétion I am going south
To ram his constitution down his mouth"?

                    (*Cheering. Dimly.*)

He's coming.

                    BRELLE

This victory should buy quiet.
Adjust my mitre and my robes, I must learn to conduct
Myself like a dutiful archbishop;
But I am too old to change.
Do I hear a trumpet?

                    SYLLA

The President has always been a vain man,
But noble as kings.

                    VASTEY

Royalty frightens him, he is otherwise intentioned.
Why do you two smile? It is as I mentioned.

    (*A sennet. Enter* CHRISTOPHE *and* LIEUTENANTS.)

Hail!

                    (*The* CROWD *echoes this.*)

Today you free your country from her enemies
With a new government cloaked in modesty
In open sunlight; peace like blackbirds
Shall settle on the season.

(*The* CROWD *applauds.*)

BRELLE

Sprinkle the conqueror with holy hope,

And pray he control the power given

By God and history to his grip. Let war adjourn; we are tired

Of bitter separations between complexions

That grin above the skeleton. All flesh is similar;

We have so little time for hooded prayers,

The eremite mercy, the black regret.

Let us live like servants

To the inspired intentions history frames today,

And pray that he directs his services straight to God

As this breath, censers, smoke, and wish

Rise crookedly to heaven. Kneel, President.

(*He blesses him.*)

Now rise gowned solely in Christian humility,

And learn from this precious silver of my eyes that I

Who should be beyond complexions

Am proud of this dark brood of sorrows

Who rise to birth from blood; but blood that must no more

    be cheap,

The currency of gain. Hold this life precious

To tell history and children remembering us in queer

    languages

By cracked columns, in dusty aisles where weeds

Are memory's signatures: our breed shall learn

How men like you, Toussaint, Brelle, Dessalines, dead,

Led their own people from embarrassment to insolence,

Breaking their former masters on their knees.
Rise and rule well, but never give cause
To turn these children against themselves and you;
Because if you do that, I shall betray you, too.
Henri, I welcome you to the uncontested presidency.

CHRISTOPHE

I cannot speak from pride.

VASTEY

Speech, speech . . .

(*The* CROWD *picks this up.*)

BRELLE

That is the politician's nightmare.
It is a wonder how they speak too often
At the wrong time, then at the right time soften.

(*Laughter.*)

CHRISTOPHE

I can only show my pride in promises;
My tongue is only garrulous
In dreams. But I will try to speak.
I have beaten Pétion; he will not trouble us.
It was a long campaign. The men, your husbands, sons, brothers,
Are tired; we all want peace;
I will send them home. I promise you my rule

Shall burst the gourds of plenty;
I will make history, richer than all kings.

BRELLE

Still plucking at an irritated string . . .
King . . . King . . .

VASTEY

Citizens, should this man not be King?
   (*The* CROWD *murmurs disappointedly.*)
Ingratitudes, so he must show his wounds,
Bare his split shoulder like a harlot, to beg the purses
Of your wish?

    (*The* CROWD *grumbles.*)

FIRST VOICE

Why must he be King? Is it an honour?

SOLDIER

But he is the liberator, and donor
Of this peace; gratitude must give her feeling voice.

SECOND VOICE

In temporary forgetting you rejoice.
I remember . . .

SOLDIER

This is history, titles and medals are toys . . .

VASTEY

Make him a king and joys shall fill your scenes
With splendour, dignity, plenty.

FIRST VOICE

With all the splendour of a Dessalines,
The palace glittering, our stomachs empty?

SYLLA

This is hardly the occasion.

BRELLE

Yet we cannot settle these things by evasion,
With candles lowering in rustling chambers;
This is a young energetic nation,
And these are not the rabble but respectable members.
What does the President say?

CHRISTOPHE

I will be King if the nation
Wants, otherwise it has not been my inclination.

BRELLE

Do you speak as a man or as a politician?

CHRISTOPHE

I speak as my country's physician,
Admitting deceptions to restore her sanity.

BRELLE

You hear him? Offer a crown.

Tear the veil of purpose from his ambition,

Try him, offer some sort of crown.

   (*The* CROWD *echoes this.*)

There is no crown. Vastey, here is my mitre.

Present it to this servant of his country,

Warn him of the implications that tighten

Around this honour that seems an only indolent office.

Only God makes kings.

   (VASTEY *offers the mitre.*)

   Wait.

When you wear this mitre's meaning on your skull,

Remember the crude riots death must stage

To amuse; it has in it the authority of the bishopric,

A mortal right over the flesh's province,

The light imprisoned in the eye, the death of tongues;

It expels the criminal and cripple without why—

That's more than I can do, and more

Than God thinks worth His doing.

With this for signature, you can

Break the built bone, make the eyes drink the dark.

Why do you hesitate? This halt is dangerous—

Why watch me so? You think I mock you, but you are my
  friend.

Because I am your friend I mock you here.

I do not like that dubious hesitation.

Does temptation make you tremble, or is it ambition creeping

Through lymph and vein like snakes to eat this offer?
That hesitation . . .
> (*Tired, he knocks the crown over.*)
The crowd sighs, Henri, with relief,
I do, too.
Return my mitre, it has made history.
Say something, Henri.

(CHRISTOPHE *passes the* CROWD *and goes to the steps to speak.*)

CHRISTOPHE

I am tired of many things,
Chief, living. This ephemeral gesture
Of a greying hero, with murders for his memory,
I think this is the tiredness
That threatened Dessalines before he died.
Leave us. Go home.
> (*The* CROWD *disperses raggedly.*)
I am very confused, Father.
> (SYLLA *and* GENERALS *go;* VASTEY *and* BRELLE *stay.*)
I had no comfort; what I wanted
Was memory, which no worm bites; this summer flesh
Wrapped in comfort around the arctic bone
Will crumble like my work; you understand, white man,
This nigger search for fame
Dragged like a meteor across my black rule.
Apart from that I have no ease,
No gods, Haitian or Christian; my primer is blood or honour;

My pieces, cathedrals that I would build,
Would have made brick biographies, green ruin,
Played over by children and girls dressed like butterflies
In a tropic summer. But you cannot understand, only Vastey.

BRELLE

You have no faith,
You want to be King.
You pray to a God of power and glory,
No prayer is answerable till hands are meek.
You think I am all faith.
Our faiths, Henri, are only crooked divers crouched
For leap into negation; spun on a world
Then flung into the dark where horror rules,
Guesses like stars whirl, hazardous in the dark;
I too doubted that only temporal triumphed.
This world is like a teardrop posed
In the eyelid of eternity, then dropping down the dark,
Round as a bubble, pricked by accident.
Accept this harm, master
The death of summer opening in the petal,
The evil threatening your light:
To be President is enough.

VASTEY

Must he break his back,
Squatting on a soldier's stool
With failing eyes? He grows old.

And now this desk, buried up to the neck
With the flat white wishes of hope turned to paper,
Dead hands, dead wishes around him,
His eyes and veins all ink?
Shame, Priest,
It is religion that is our confusion.

BRELLE

I know you both bitterly resent my intrusion,
But I know the emptiness of glory;
It is not the amount of syllables that make the story
But the sincerity.
You think my intrusion to be severity:
I have risen from acolyte to archbishop.
You from a slave in Grenada to this grandeur.
Where is the honour? Pardon me, Henri.

CHRISTOPHE

A man does not like to be brought naked in the sun,
Or have his hopes pilloried in the market.
Leave us, Brelle.

(BRELLE *goes out.*)

My dreams are cracked, scudded like smoke.

VASTEY

I tried my best. I should have had
More accomplices in the crowd:
That soldier was not loud.

CHRISTOPHE

You did your best.

There will be another chance.

I will be King, a king flows in me. I am tired;

Let us go in.

To ride through shouts, crowned, insolent, to ride

Under long arches.

VASTEY (*Leading him away.*)

Yes, General.

We must try again.

CHRISTOPHE (*Laughing.*)

There is no "more."

The leaves rust in silence; rivers and tongues

Are dry; my age is drought:

Grey hairs and wrinkles and the senile clutch

Of one dry grief to the anarchy of the bough.

That's how I feel, but to be King, only to be King; ah, Vastey,

To rule in comfort . . . ah . . .

Let us go in.

    (*They are going out, when they hear the* CROWD.)

The crowd, their laughter, huge childish terrors,

Like a river's noise in history.

Do not trust crowds, Vastey,

Break them or they break you.

   (*They go out. For a moment the stage is bare, the bunting
and flags draping mockery when the* CROWD *returns.*)

SOLDIER

And this gratitude we pay him? Shame!

FIRST VOICE

Honour and love are rich enough estates
For any.

SECOND VOICE

It is certain that he is a good soldier,
Loves his country; but why crave
The crown and its dangers?

FIRST VOICE

We saw what the sceptre did to Dessalines;
Do we want that repeated?

SOLDIER

Rubbish. Dessalines is dead and Pétion is defeated;
No crow rules but a king
Who is king except in name only.

FIRST VOICE

Then that should content him.

(*Laughter and jeering.*)

SOLDIER (*Establishing quiet.*)

Is it for that in fear you sent him,
To wear his wounds without reward,

Mocked in the market, the pawn of peasants?
I am a soldier and love his service,
Dwell in his discipline without desertion.
Hand him the crown in a revised assertion,
Crown him with clemency, not in derision.
I say all this, what is your decision?

FIRST VOICE

Why should a king's name honour him further?

SOLDIER

You let Dessalines rule and he was despotic,
You are helpless, and numb in the narcotic
Of your superstitions. Only a king can rule;
Give your government dignity. Must it look like a
    school
Conducted by a foolish master?

SECOND VOICE

Oh, if the crown comfort him, let him have it.

(*They cheer.*)

SOLDIER

He is born to be king; he will build
A weather only of wealth. Call him.

(*Some go off.*)

FIRST VOICE

Remember, Dessalines . . .

SECOND VOICE

How much are you getting
For what you are repeating?

SOLDIER

Oh, shut up.

FIRST VOICE

Remember that power changes the powerful.
Here is your King . . .
     (*Re-enter* CHRISTOPHE *and* VASTEY.)
All smiles; like prisoners, they break
The prison of restraint and modesty.

SOLDIER

Speak quickly, fool, or you speak anarchy after this.
They cry for you, Your Majesty; fear made them hesitate
To honour you with your natural estate.
General, you are now King; they are fickle;
Abuse the sickle, opportunity,
In harvest. Look, he cannot speak; leave him.
Let us leave.
    (*The* CROWD *goes, bewildered. The* SOLDIER *hesitates, then*
                  is paid. Exiting.)
Goodbye, Your Majesty.

CHRISTOPHE

Poor Brelle.
I think they love me.

VASTEY

That soldier did it; we must fatten him.
He never gives up, he would fight
With a sword's stub.

CHRISTOPHE

Their love goes further than the corporal.
So, I am King.

VASTEY

Pétion is powerful still in the south,
A king rules this country in the blue north;
This is the richer side of Haiti; look at the hills
Curled in the afternoon like mist.

CHRISTOPHE

On that blue smoking citadel
That hides the sun until its zenith by its height,
I will build a fort
Made out of stone, as befits a soldier,
Magnificent in marble, a king's comfort.
So high, so bleak,
The sound of the sea will be only a weak wind, or to look
Down on the summer sea, spreading sleep
In wrinkles, will giddy.

VASTEY

At what cost will the general build these things?
Bishoprics oppose the caprices of kings.

CHRISTOPHE

Caprices! Who talks of caprices?
I will exhaust this country into riches. Have you seen
The contagion of blight settling on the limes like apathy
On our stalks? I will build my cathedral in a month,
Then break or build this kingdom.
Look, look up, that hill . . .

VASTEY

That one, where the gulls achieve halfway,
Then slide back screaming to a muttering sea?
I see; why?

CHRISTOPHE

The air is thin there, the balding rocks
Where the last yellow grass clutch whitening in sun,
And the steep pass below the sea, knocking
Like a madman on the screaming sand,
And the wind howling down the precipices like a lunatic
Searching a letter he never wrote—against these rocks,
Wind, sand, cold, where the sharp cry of gulls beats faintly
    on the ears,
And in the green grove a milk of doves—what army
Would bend its head against the wind to reach?
We would, there, be safe.

And strong, and pretty.
The smell of roses which the sea wind dispels,
Dispelling also the birds' voice, the weaker oleander—
Let us build white-pointed citadels,
Crusted with white perfections over
This epilogue of Eden, a prosperous Haiti,
My kingdom where I, a king, rule.
Mine, mine, Vastey! Once a slave,
Then after that Napoleon can envy,
With the Antilles mine, the whole archipelago overturning
Cauldrons of history and violence on their masters' heads,
The slaves, the kings, the blacks, the brave.

VASTEY

A king only is strong,
A king alone rules long,
And a king's children.

CHRISTOPHE

I shall build châteaux
That shall obstruct the strongest season,
So high the hawk shall giddy in its gyre
Before it settles on the carved turrets.
My floors shall reflect the face that passes over them,
And foreign trees spread out the shade of government
On emerald lawns; I will hold councils.
I'll pave a room with golden coins, so rich
The old archbishop will smile indulgently at heaven from
The authenticity of my châteaux.

I will have Arabian horses, yellow-haired serving boys,
And in the night the châteaux will be lit
With lanterns bewildering as fireflies,
Over the lawns at night, like mobile candelabra.
I who was a slave am now a king; after my strength
Not England, Jamaica, or Napoleon
Shall send ships to disgorge invasions, but search for
Trade and quiet. Haiti will flourish,
When I am King.

VASTEY (*Yawning.*)

It is going to rain.
Let us go in.
It is beginning to get dark.

(*Fade-out.*)

Scene 2

The throne room in the palace. It is dark, VASTEY *and an*
ATTENDANT *enter; there is the sound of church music from*
an adjacent room.

VASTEY

Strike a light.
Where is this music? Oh, the château chapelle . . .
Brelle is at prayer. Here it is so dark,
But bowed at his altars in bowers of brightness,
An archbishop praying with shortening wax,

Rehearsing his death by muttering martyrdoms,
Unravelling litanies of murdered saints—
The fool.
That lovely music! Mournful, meditative . . .

ATTENDANT

Shall I light a candle?

VASTEY

Wait. This music is appropriate to this dark,
Spreading, like silken water, ripples of quiet.
Strike a light? I told you, go on.

ATTENDANT

Yes, sir.

VASTEY

Strange how this glare reflects a dancing
Of my will that will not be stilled.
Light knocks and flickers on the wall . . .
Are you sure the King's not here?

ATTENDANT

Yes, sir. I thought it was the archbishop you wanted.

VASTEY

I will get the archbishop . . .
Is it true the soldiers are shedding

Their duties shyly, like dirty suits?
No, light no more chances; is it true
The few that remain threaten faction?
How much of this rebellion is rumour?

ATTENDANT

I don't know, Baron.

VASTEY

I waited for that . . .
And when will you desert us,
And be pawned to Pétion for his promise of plenty?
What do the people think of the King?
Certainly the priest is better liked?
Speak up, you can only be shot . . .

ATTENDANT

They like everybody, sir.
We like the King . . .

VASTEY

Where is the chapel door?
You say the King will not come here?

ATTENDANT

No, sir.
The chapel door is two doors after.

VASTEY

Here are two letters. Can you read?
No? Put these in slyness in the bishop's vestments
While he is whispering hypocrisies to heaven
With penny candles humble in his eyes,
Turning pages of meditation with dry rustling lips.
He must not know about the letters.
He will take time to pray, more than an hour . . .
Hide them where you can find them, because you will take
Them back, to show the King.
Lock question on your lips, lackeys do not quarrel;
It will do the priest no harm.
You cannot read?

ATTENDANT

No . . . no, sir . . .

VASTEY

Do not be awkward; there are
Several kings who cannot.
When will the King come?

ATTENDANT

I think I hear him . . .

VASTEY

I know he likes to sprawl, wasting his energy walking in
    the dark,
Thinking his power far into the dark,

Or is it regret that thrusts him in the dark,
Out of society?
Look, hurry, be quiet, numb to suspicion; and efficient.
I hear a step . . .

(*Exit* ATTENDANT. VASTEY *lights another candle as*
CHRISTOPHE *enters.*)

CHRISTOPHE

That chapelle music—
The architectural arabesque halts, spreads, builds
In vision; when I hear madrigals, requiems,
It is so much like constructing citadels, châteaux,
Or, sometimes, Vastey, in the labyrinth brain,
The theme runs out its threads like—who was it—Theseus,
That book you read me, descending down the spirals of the
    ear;
Then, listen, a crash, crescendo comes, like urge, like knock
    of light
Burst from the petal and the bud's green prison,
Like glare of sun, or like a minotaur;
Then hear it dying, the thread lost, the light broken, the
    metal leaf
Rusted with time; and who was it—Theseus
Travelling out of light and knowledge like the bone,
Complexions of the skeleton.
My thoughts tease death, Vastey;
I am getting old.

VASTEY

All of us, Henri.
Even Brelle.

CHRISTOPHE

Poor Brelle.
And Sylla—dead, eh?

VASTEY

You ask me often; he was an old man.

CHRISTOPHE

My friend, they say that old men die
Mumbling a syntax of the probable;
Truth breaks, refractory on their days of dark,
Like chips of moon, lavish on their death edge . . .

VASTEY

He was always talking about the moon, and death,
Also regret . . .
His own white-haired regret
Was the anatomy that he wore to the grave,
Always regretting what his mad youth did,
A spendthrift general spilling coins of blood
Around the altars of the god of pity.
Surely you are not regretting
Taking Brelle's advice?

CHRISTOPHE (*Flaring briefly.*)

No, damn it.

Anyway, he died, broken, grey, and quiet,

White-haired as the moon and stumbling just as lost

Through peace-fleeced colonies of clouds, a foolish, mad
    old man.

VASTEY

But quiet, safe. Dead.

CHRISTOPHE

Yes, archbishops live.

They whom the gods love die young . . .

He is at chapel now, isn't he?

VASTEY

Or perhaps plotting piety with Pétion.

Or receiving letters from the south . . .

CHRISTOPHE (*Anger mounting.*)

What insanity are you talking?

You do not like Brelle. Why?

VASTEY

Do you, Your Majesty?

Sixty years of conscience on a mangy martyr

White and superior as his Paris statues?

His obvious love for clear complexions,

His pride in Pétion, his dislike
Of being repeatedly contradicted?
Oh, certainly I like him, equally,
As you or Dessalines.

CHRISTOPHE

Do not mention Dessalines
And I in the same breath.
How do you know?

VASTEY

Search his vestments, he kneels in the chapel,
Break at his pride while he mumbles mercies
To black baboons who wear king's clothes . . .

CHRISTOPHE

Whom are you referring to?

VASTEY

That is how
He feels, I have heard him . . .

CHRISTOPHE

But those letters . . .
His vestments . . . It is below me to search . . .
Pétion?

VASTEY

I have not eaten yet . . .

CHRISTOPHE

What?

VASTEY

My supper. May I leave?

CHRISTOPHE

Of course, of course . . . Letters . . .
As you go, send in a soldier or a servingman.
I will find out . . .

VASTEY

Yes . . . You know the postmark of the south,
I need not be here to read it.

(*He exits.*)

CHRISTOPHE

Archbishop, if this is true,
I will kill you with these hands that have known
To forget vocabulary of blood . . .
Your life, Brelle, is nothing more
Than candle stubs, or incense dying with a sign in
    censers,
And you already a tired, weak old fool,
Too keen and political
And overfat with conscience . . .
You will see how I value lives . . . then talk to angels
When I draw out a dagger;
Then call your God.

We men are helpless, accident our religion,
Birth, death, and life are accident . . .
After the mathematics of casualty
We are still children guessing after dark,
Waiting for dim collisions of spectrum-splintered stars;
Birth breaks around the lips, children learning language of
  error.
Your death, Archbishop, would
Be accident.
Ah, Brelle, our God is no more than a guess,
A hoax of heaven, a nun's nicety;
Time is the god that breaks us on his knees, learning
Our ruin and repeating epitaphs
Like a dull pupil; it is that one that flings
That moon, a wild white spinning coin in grooves of time;
But death returns as the bright thrown dust falls, and
  walks
Into the memory, the death, the dark.
            (*Enter the* ATTENDANT.)
Good, you are here.
Do you know the chapel?
Good. Search the archbishop's clothes, then bring
Me letters, paper. Look well,
And bring it quietly; keep
This business dark.
            (*The* ATTENDANT *exits.*)
The time is full of poison—
Cunning in the cup and lies in the linen;
So this is kingship, vermin among the vows,

Traitors in surplices and swords in tongues . . .
This rule is only to the violent man.
     (*Re-enter* ATTENDANT *with the letters.*)
Ah.
They want to plot against my monarch's love.
Can you read?

ATTENDANT

No, Your Majesty.

CHRISTOPHE

This letter is from the south, isn't it?

ATTENDANT

The stamp looks so; it has the seal.

CHRISTOPHE (*Angrily*)

I cannot read it. But what if it is
A trick of Vastey's?
The archbishop treacherous! Who would believe it?
Send him to me, I'll find out.
     (*As the* ATTENDANT *goes,* BRELLE *enters.*)
Welcome, Your Grace.
I wanted to see you.

BRELLE

You mock the Church that warmed your head with oil.
Your attendant preceded my own intentions;
I wanted to talk with you.

Henri, you must stop these insolences to decency,
Frame a just constitution or face calamity.
Pétion is massing his military in the south,
And generals desert you slyly every dusk;
The peasants have made small active agitations
Which by sheer brutality your forces split,
But you have scattered sparks from the hard anvil,
And the country waits to pull down
Narrow castles, citadels, and make a passage of war.
You drive the peasants without mercy. Do you consider
    mercy?
Have you no bitter memory to depose
Your cruelty from its holiday at the blood's bright money?
And now you force your poison to my clergy,
Corrupting with gold, corroding with silver.
God, what a waste of blood, these cathedrals, castles, built;
Bones in the masonry, skulls in the architrave,
Tired masons falling from the chilly turrets.
Henri, you must stop.
I prayed for you,
Only a humble old man.

CHRISTOPHE

Is this what you
Have come here to threaten?

BRELLE

The King's law is the Church's care;
And as long as you rule badly

The Church must war against this evil; sadly
I, who am your enemy, am your friend;
You oppose my flock and rape my pastorate
To glut your lusts: I cannot stand for this . . .

CHRISTOPHE (*With mounting anger*)
                                    Stand?
You cannot stand for this? You speak to the one who is here
To stand for this black country; it is not yours to stand
Or understand. I am the King, I am the state,
I shall work for the state as I am King
Against what any archbishop will stand for.

BRELLE
Then there will always be strife
Between us; there will always be the knife
Dividing the spiritual from the temporal,
Dividing even to the point of blood . . .

CHRISTOPHE
Look here, white man, do you threaten me?

BRELLE
Or perhaps my blood, as you killed Dessalines.

CHRISTOPHE
I killed Dessalines and you smiled.

BRELLE (*Softly*)

I have not been a good priest.
But I was not archbishop then, and only blood
Could buy this comfort, and your graph to authority.
I was a poor priest,
But then I wanted too much; that is why
To stop is better, Henri, than to waste. No one will pity.
I am old, and act
In this arena of sanity; my purposes are broad and open
As the blue air. This is the ambition
That drives me to the ground with hard grey hairs;
I toyed and threatened God, demanding more than a
    simple death and life.
You think me hypocrite; I wanted honour, comfort
Beyond this muttering in the dark; that was the hope
I had before time put on wrinkles, and now I wear
The stubborn motley of a peevish priest.
Henri, we are fools.

CHRISTOPHE

What about these letters?
What about Pétion?

BRELLE

I hear many rumours.

CHRISTOPHE

I can kill rumours easily;
You only have to throw a threat in their direction

And tongues and fears fly up like a throw of birds;
Suspicions and plots are easily brought to light:
Truth crouches in the dark.
The letters . . .

BRELLE *(Cautiously)*

What have they to do with me?

CHRISTOPHE

Who said anything?

BRELLE

Come, come, Henri, what new plot is this?

CHRISTOPHE

But I refuse to be caught by you into accusing.
My accusation would mean only your refusing,
Then what?
     (He gestures in mock helplessness.)

BRELLE

What am I supposed to have done?
Write these letters?
Whose idea, Vastey's?

CHRISTOPHE *(Bewildered)*

Ah . . .

BRELLE

What am I guilty of?

CHRISTOPHE

Choose any treason.

BRELLE

I have one chronic treason
Which no death can eat, and that is love.

CHRISTOPHE

I am not a civilised man, Father;
I am at heart very primitive; there is that urge—
A beast in the jungle among primitive angers
Clawing down opposition; what is the expression—
The instinct?

BRELLE

I do not know.
I know only this love
I have for peace, religion, and the suffering people.

CHRISTOPHE (*Tearing the letters, screaming.*)

Oh, shut that hypocrite heart,
Gabbling of love while you mock our complexions,
Inviting death to grow taller after dying;
You wrote those letters, are guilty of treason.
Old man, you have arrived at the end of a season;
I rule now. Take your hoax,

Your statues, and your warnings, and blessing saints
Out of my house, and Haiti.

BRELLE

This is the curse of the nation,
Eating your own stomach, where the sickness is;
Your smell of blood offends the nostrils of God.

CHRISTOPHE

Perhaps the smell of sweat under my arms
Offend that God, too, quivering His white crooked nostrils.
Well, tell Him after death that it is honest
As the seven words of blood broken on His flesh; tell Him
The nigger smell, that even kings must wear,
Is bread and wine to life.
I am proud, I have worked and grown
This country to its stature: tell Him that.

BRELLE

With hammer and hatred breaking
What Toussaint built, exploding
Where he created. How many dead
Children has your love considered?
Will you never learn the lesson
You taught your best friend in the grammar death?
You broke his breath like a stalk; and now you walk,
A subtle monster lost in rooms of himself;
Your hate walks out of screens
With fifty murders smiling in its hand.

You have become worse than your Dessalines;
You have grown mad with satisfaction and despair.
How long, King, will you continue to wear
A cloak of blood around an ex-slave shoulder?

CHRISTOPHE

Slave, eh? You have never forgotten that.
Will that never dissolve?
I have not a conscience but a memory.
Brelle, you have gone too far.

BRELLE (*Feeling his success.*)

Not far enough.
We must all suffer, even you, eh, King?
The anatomy of pity, the pearl of pain, is common suffering.
A unity of wounds transcends the agony.
Think how the world is suffering and you will smile;
Think how so many kings were killed and you will feel
    lucky.
You think a slave is shame . . .
When I was in a seminary in Provence,
Meditating martyrdom among the poplars,
I thought and toyed of a bright martyrdom,
Selling my faith for death, to blacks . . .

CHRISTOPHE

I have told you myself
Not to refer contemptuously to my people.

BRELLE

They are my people too, King,
And they are black;
Spiritual power has never made me despotic,
As temporal power has made you insane, neurotic;
What kind of perverse kindness is it that denies
Them white bread but will not let a friend call them blacks?

CHRISTOPHE

You say it again,
Priest. I am tired of your complexion;
I have had too much to do with this.
Besides, you talk to no slave . . .

BRELLE

And you to God's elect,
An archbishop.

CHRISTOPHE

Because of my rule, and Dessalines's dying.

BRELLE

What black ignorance in king and country . . .

CHRISTOPHE

Provoking me . . .
But why?
What comfort is your death,

Perhaps you think . . . Oh, I see
Rebellion, a trick with you and Pétion?

BRELLE

You are so lost.
Good night.

    (BRELLE *is going. He passes contemptuously by*
CHRISTOPHE. *The stabbing is quiet and terrible, with a*
minimum amount of struggle.)

CHRISTOPHE

What fools! Assembling on the shelves of their lives
Clay gods, and in a dusty room,
Half-broken faiths that falsify,
Building their need for comfort into religions!
The one final thing is death, and how you die. I die crowned!
And you, white man,
This death beats dying; I have built
These châteaux of my past that no time eats.
A slave, I survive.
Vastey . . . Vastey . . .

VASTEY (*Who has been near.*)

Yes, Henri.

CHRISTOPHE

We are safe now.

VASTEY

I know.

CHRISTOPHE

We have strangled memory and regret,
But this must be the last.
I nearly could not kill him, but when he said . . .
What drums are those?
They are coming nearer.
Oh, Vastey, my dreams . . .
Ruin, ruin, O King, ruin and blood!
Someone has blown out the candle of the sun.
Ruin and blood.
Stain my eyes, my linen, I walked alone in a wood
Of skeletons and thorns where the leaves dripped blood.
Get this mess cleaned.
Do you hear drums?

VASTEY

Forget. Try to sleep;
We are safe, you talk like old Sylla.
What do you hear? The wind, that lost ghost
Under the willows, with a thread for a voice; only
The wind; I hear it, too.
Do you think it is Pétion?

CHRISTOPHE

Ah, who is Pétion? . . .
I want to sleep.

VASTEY

Yes.

You know they really sound like drums . . .

What's the matter?

CHRISTOPHE

My legs, my legs . . .

I always get these pains . . .

A cramp I cannot stab away.

Help me to the throne: it will pass.

(*Fade-out.*)

Scene 3

The scene is the same as before. It is dim. CHRISTOPHE,
*wearing only his general's cloak, torn open to show
his bare chest, is sprawled on the throne, muttering
to himself.* VASTEY, *near the throne, is watching
a* WITCH DOCTOR *fuss over skull and incense in
an elaborate, unconvincing ritual.*

VASTEY

How are our legs now?

CHRISTOPHE

I cannot move them . . .

VASTEY

Henri, we must leave the citadel,
Pétion is already a day near;
Even here, La Ferrière, is not safe.
You must . . .

CHRISTOPHE

I know, I know.
                    (*He indicates the* WITCH DOCTOR.)
What is he doing?
Tell him to stop praying to wooded mercies and get
Me erect; tell him it is useless.
Christ and Damballa, or any god . . .

VASTEY

Wooden gods, they are not much good;
If I stocked all the superstitions end to end,
Or let now a crooked prayer climb, no god
Would excuse guilt.

CHRISTOPHE

Tell him to try again the rub, that mixture,
The old herbs, the antique magic,
That breed abortions; the weeds and smoking herbs
    cropped,
Hemlock-harmful, lethe-lulling,
Flowers of forgetting, raped from their cradles
In smoke, mists, and weathers . . .

VASTEY

He says it is wrong to rub you again so soon.

CHRISTOPHE

Ah . . . tell him to go.

VASTEY (*Touching the* WITCH DOCTOR.)
Allez.

CHRISTOPHE

Ask him to leave the skull and incense . . .
But go, with his gods and their wooden smiles . . .
　　　　　(*The* WITCH DOCTOR *goes.*)
Well, Brelle is dead . . .

VASTEY

I stumbled on his sprawled pride in the corridor,
He has his martyrdom.
No one to bury him. We are alone now.
Pétion powerful, Sylla silent.
Dessalines dead, Christophe . . . cramped . . .
This cramp, where is it?

CHRISTOPHE (*Irritated*)

How many times must I say?
I don't know; all over.

VASTEY

My own paralysis
Creeps somewhere between my will
And my regret. There are broken statues
On my tongue, dead stale civilizations
Breeding in my brain. You, if you could walk,
You could see the citadel, the soldiers have left it.
There is dust settling on the armoury,
Shafted beams with dust rising like history in the chapel,
Cracked windows and the vocabulary of ruin
Littered on lawns; the gardens and menagerie, the
     oleander
Groves, dead or rotten.

CHRISTOPHE

But regret,
Why do you regret?

VASTEY

For two days, with your paralysis,
I have lived in my huge linen rooms, eating my fears
Like the worm gnawing on the corner
Of the shroud of silence;
Drinking remorse in a spoonful of soup.
Dust on the mirrors, and floors cracking . . .
When I think of the past.
God!

CHRISTOPHE

You cannot stop gabbling?
If I had legs, and an army . . .

VASTEY

And Pétion is coming waving a new constitution.
Ragged herds follow. Oh, if he knew, or they,
How they were marching tall into the grave, murders,
    fevers,
And what responsibility the crown tightens.
Oh God, Henri!

CHRISTOPHE

Do not call gods, Vastey.
The gods are monstered children; they build
To break, or history
Burning biographies like rubbish, while time
Carries their smoke like memory past the nostrils.
Those who die hoping are grey children;
So death, selling his wares,
Fooled the archbishop.

VASTEY

But, as you said of Sylla,
He is safe now. Dead with dignity.

CHRISTOPHE

He was white.

VASTEY

In death, Henri, the bone is anonymous;
Complexions only grin above the skeleton;
Under the grass the dust is an anthology of creeds and skins.
Who can tell what that skull was?
Was it for that we quarreled?

CHRISTOPHE

Yes, fool; for that Haiti bled,
And spilled the valuable aristocratic blood
To build these citadels for this complexion
Signed by the sun.
Yes, for that we killed, because some were black,
And some were spat on.
For that I overturned the horn of plenty,
And harvest grey hairs and calumny;
It is I who, history, gave them this voice to shout anarchy
Against the King. I made this King they hate,
Shaped out of slaves . . .
What have I done, what have I done, Vastey, to deserve all
    this?

VASTEY

Dessalines, Brelle,
The violent love of self that kills the self.
Cathedrals and cruelties;
The apocalypse horsemen riding down starving ranks;
Thanks, thanks, thanks,
Forced to the King from bleeding lips;

Cannon and cruelty poured from the sides of ships.
Oh, Henri, we are guilty; admit, admit, it's time.

CHRISTOPHE

How dare you assume
Such a familiar tone?
The only unguent I can rub on these bones
Is I have done what I would do again.

VASTEY

Is it not possible that you are sinking
In a quicksand of safety, thinking
Corruptions safe as the sand closes? It is not your house
You must put in order but yourself.

CHRISTOPHE

You take advantage while I am weak;
If I could flog these limbs to action—
(*The drums beat faintly, and the action, dim as it is, petrifies
them both.* CHRISTOPHE *withdraws, slowly, a pistol from
hiding, then settles it more accessibly.*)
Pétion is powerful. They are coming,
They are coming, Vastey.
If I could move . . .

VASTEY

You cannot tell how near they are,
And it is thickening,
And the châteaux are tall and dark. I must hide. I must hide.

The light . . .
Now it is dark.
This is the room where Brelle, with music playing . . .
Hither a new king, and another archbishop,
Monotonies of history . . .
We are finished, Majesty,
We were a tragedy of success.

CHRISTOPHE

It was not a great life, Vastey,
But the dying compensates it:
No slave, but a king
Whose exhalation is signed with meteors,
Whose spilled blood canonizes its anarchy.
Think of Brelle's eyes with nothing in the pupils,
His hands contorted on a crooked crucifix,
Redemption, not riot, on his dusty lips;
And consider how confessions, penultimate pieties,
Are comical or forced. I cannot regret,
I acted evenly.
And I was often happy.

VASTEY

Happy, Henri?
Then no contritions?

(CHRISTOPHE *picks up the pistol absently as the drums
mount in tension.*)

CHRISTOPHE

Happiness is sensual, my equerry;
The fine meal, and the ready wife, the smile
Between the waltzes and cadenzas, the leap of lechery
In the wild ropes and rivers of the thighs.
Grief with despair, ruin, the crack of time,
Wreckage of several lives around our ankles, these lives
Are hopes the sea rejects; time's tidal griefs
Rock with the moon's knock, waves wreck our wraths,
Hopes drown, and kings fade on the memory.
These are the hard truths we cannot eat,
The black anarchy of the night, with dawn
Bleeding from its edges like a wound; the straw you
    hold,
Whether it is religion, fame, or hope, the kiss, the dying
    action,
Made by a huge mimer in an empty hall—
All these are the rich agony of living.
We wait, with accident our mercy, and truth is pain;
And pain, like joy, is sensual; so to feel happy, Vastey,
Is nothing; it is to chew half
Of our globe and spit truth out in morsels,
Those bitter truths that choke the craw of hopes.
I have no regret, and happiness?
Well, end the sermon.
The drums have stopped.
They are here.
The light, strengthen the light,
I will not die in the dark.

VASTEY

It is almost morning.

Tomorrow has no comfort; we must wage war against the dark

In all of us, and make our chaos light.

Regret, King, time . . .

(CHRISTOPHE *laughs loudly,* VASTEY *signals quiet.*)

CHRISTOPHE

Regret, and your knees knocking?

(*His laughter dies.*)

That silence. Why have they stopped? They are here.

I can hear them, Vastey.

(*His gun is drawn.*)

VASTEY (*Tense, whispering*)

But you cannot tell where—

CHRISTOPHE (*Bewildered and angry*)

Yes, yes, I can tell . . .

VASTEY

How near are they?

(*A resounding crash, like glass, then silence.*)

What was that now?

CHRISTOPHE

The Hall of Mirrors.

If I could move . . .

(He forces himself half upright facing the direction of the noise. VASTEY*, behind him, retreats slowly, until he is out of sight.* CHRISTOPHE*, unaware that he is alone, is speaking half to himself.)*

Do not regret, Vastey.

But why do they stop playing? You say it will soon be
morning . . .

Why do they stop? Vastey?

(He turns around.)

Vastey . . .

*(He sinks in the chair, beaten, but alert, muttering, watching
the skull and the incense in the foreground.)*

I am not without pity, but pity comes tardily, and fits
Raggedly around my crimes. Besides, I think,
In honesty, I am rather sorrier
For myself than all those things I did.
I cannot ripen compunction by rosaries
Or pray to Damballa, or broken gods.

(A scream. VASTEY *is taken.* CHRISTOPHE *hardly listens.)*

History, breaking the stalk she grew herself,
Kills us like flies, wings torn, held up to light,
Burning biographies like rubbish.

(He addresses the skull.)

Skull, when your smile wore flesh around its teeth,
Time like a pulse was knocking in the eyelid,
The worm was mining in the bone for metal.
What shall I leave?
I am alone . . . this anonymous skull?

What shall I? . . . A half-charred name?
No. A king's memory, or oblivion.
>   (*The drums rise, and he struggles to his feet,*
>   *shouting to be heard.*)
Tell Pétion I leave him this dark monarchy,
The graves of children, and years of silence . . .
>   (*His voice breaks with laughter and despair.*)
And after that . . .
Oblivion and silence.
>   (*The drums reach their pitch, and when they stop suddenly,*
>   *he shudders at the silence and puts the pistol slowly to his*
>   *head as . . . the curtain falls.*)

DRUMS AND COLOURS

Drums and Colours was produced in the Botanical Gardens, Port of Spain, Trinidad, on April 25, 1958. It was commissioned to mark the opening of the first West Indies Federation. The play was directed by Noel Vaz and Dagmar Butt. Costumes were designed by Motley. Lighting by John Robertson.

The cast was as follows:

CHORUS—*Leonard St. Hill*

EMMANUEL MANO—*Errol Jones*

POMPEY—*James King*

YETTE—*Jean Herbert*

RAM—*Freddie Kissoon*

GENERAL YU—*Mills Olivier*

LAS CASAS—*Reginald Carter*

BOBADILLA—*Errol Protain*

QUADRADO—*Michael Wickers*

CHRISTOPHER COLUMBUS—*Hugh Butt*

FERNANDO—*Robert Head*

BARTOLOME—*Peter Pitts*

GARCÍA—*Conrad Gonzalez*

YOUNG PACO—*Charles Blakeman*

BROKER—*Vernon Gomez*

BROKER'S NEPHEW—*George Prichett*

PACO—*Easton Lee*

JEW—*Peter Ireson*

MERCHANT—*Henri Perrin*

SPANISH WOMEN—*Yolande Achong, Pat Cansfield, Gene Miles, Mavis Roodal*

FIRST SPANISH SAILOR—*Abraham Chami*

SECOND SPANISH SAILOR—*Asaad Sabeeney*

MALE SLAVE—*William Webb*

FEMALE SLAVE—*Eunice Bruno*

AFRICAN KING—*Horace Burgess*

PACO AS AN OLD MAN—*Ronald Williams*

YOUNG RALEIGH—*Peter Donnegan*

HUMPHREY GILBERT—*Arthur Webb*

SIR WALTER RALEIGH—*Anthony Selman*

LAURENCE KEYMIS—*William Stevenson*

DE BERRIO—*Sydney Hill*

RALEIGH'S SON—*Peter Minshall*

ENGLISH SAILORS—*Robert Head, George Prichett*

BARBADIAN WINE STEWARD—*Horace James*

PRIEST—*Errol Protain*

EXECUTIONER—*Joe Hatem*

GENERAL LECLERC—*Tom Burley*

PAULINE LECLERC—*Rhona Angel*

GENERAL DE ROUVRAY—*Pip Angel*

MADAME DE ROUVRAY—*Nancy Richards*

ARMAND CALIXTE-BREDA—*Ronald Llanos*

ANTON CALIXTE—*Desmond Rostant*

TOUSSAINT L'OVERTURE—*Neville Hall*

LIEUTENANT FOUJADE—*Peter Ireson*

BOUKMANN—*Jeff Henry*

DESSALINES—*Errol Hill*

CHRISTOPHE—*Lloyd Stanford*

HAITIAN SOLDIER—*Geoffrey Biddeau*

DEACON SALE—*A. L. Jolly*

AARON—*Winston Gay*

ELIJAH—*Bertrand Henry*

BRITISH SERGEANT—*Victor Hogg*

GEORGE WILLIAM GORDON—*Errol Protain*

CAPTAIN—*James Draper*

CALICO—*Peter Pitts*

Author's Note

In one or two instances, for purposes of thematic cohesion, I have rearranged dates and incidents, but the general pattern of discovery, conquest, exploitation, rebellion, and constitutional advancement has been followed. The play, fully performed, runs well over three hours; however, the scenes are so arranged that interested producers can excise shorter, self-contained plays from the main work, for example, the story of Paco, the El Dorado theme in the Raleigh scenes, the betrayal of Toussaint, the relationship with M. Calixte-Breda (in which the young Anton becomes the central figure), and the escapades of Pompey. I have made a few alterations and several cuts from the acting script.

D.W.

Trinidad, 1960

CAST OF PRINCIPAL CHARACTERS

CHORUS, *a Carnival figure*

EMMANUEL MANO, *a masquerader, leader of a Carnival band*

POMPEY, *a masquerader in Mano's band*

YETTE, *a masquerader in Mano's band*

RAM, *a masquerader in Mano's band*

GENERAL YU, *a masquerader in Mano's band*

LAS CASAS, *a Spanish cleric*

BOBADILLA, *governor of Santo Domingo*

QUADRADO, *a conquistador*

CHRISTOPHER COLUMBUS

FERNANDO, *a Spanish sailor*

BARTOLOME, *a Spanish sailor*

GARCÍA, *a Spanish sailor*

YOUNG PACO, *an Indian boy*

PACO, *an Indian*

A JEW, *emigrant to the New World*

A SLAVE

A FEMALE SLAVE

YOUNG RALEIGH

YOUNG GILBERT

SIR WALTER RALEIGH, *English adventurer*

SIR HUMPHREY GILBERT, *English adventurer*

LAURENCE KEYMIS, *officer of Raleigh's expedition*

DE BERRIO, *Spanish governor of Trinidad*

WINE STEWARD, *a Barbadian house slave*

GENERAL LECLERC, *French commander in Haiti*

PAULINE LECLERC, *his wife*

GENERAL DE ROUVRAY, *a French general*

CALIXTE-BREDA, *a plantation owner*

ANTON CALIXTE, *his illegitimate son*

TOUSSAINT L'OUVERTURE, *Calixte-Breda's coachman, then liberator of Haiti*

BOUKMANN, *a slave*

HENRI CHRISTOPHE, *a Haitian general*

JEAN JACQUES DESSALINES, *a Haitian general*

DEACON SALE, *a Jamaican cleric*

GEORGE WILLIAM GORDON, *a Jamaican*

Also, SPANISH WOMEN, SLAVES, SAILORS, SOLDIERS

PROLOGUE

The stage is set with a centrepiece of regimental and African
drums, with the flags of Britain, France, Spain, and Holland.
In the background, a central balcony with steps leading up to
it from either side of the stage. A distant bugle and drum roll,
then faint sounds of carnival music. The lights come up.
Enter YETTE, RAM, YU, POMPEY, *running, led by* MANO.
They rummage among set properties and dress.

MANO

Ram, Pompey, Yette, Yu, like I hear them coming.
I got a plan, boys, we going change round the carnival.
They bound to pass this alley, like I hear them approaching.
Position yourself, we going ambush this road march!

(*Enter* CARNIVAL MASKERS: *dancing.*)

MANO

Arawaks, Ashanti, Conquistadors!
Give them the bugle, Pomps!
We changing the march now to "War and Rebellion"!

(POMPEY *blows bugle: quiet. The* CROWD *objects. Shouts.*)

VOICE

Ain't that Pompey the shoemaker?

POMPEY

Is Pompey the warrior starting from today,
And I want all you listen to what I go' say.
                    (*Climbing on a barrel.*)
This confusion going change to a serious play!

(*Shouts, etc.*)

YETTE

If anyone contradict what General Pompey said,
A bullet from this musket, Pomps, go ahead.

POMPEY (*Singing.*)
Now you men of every creed and class,
We know you is brothers when you playing Mass,
White dance with black, black with Indian,
But long time, it was Rebellion.
No matter what you colour now is steel and drums,
We jumping together with open arms,
But if you listen now, you going see
The painful birth of democracy.
For in them days it was . . .

CROWD (*Singing and dancing.*)

*Bend the angle on them is to blow them down, is to blow them
   down.*

*Bend the angle on them is to blow them down, is to blow them
   down,*

When the bayonet charge is the rod of correction,

Shout it everyone: when the bayonet charge

Is the rod of correction, till rebellion!

MANO

All you get the idea, so le' we get organise now.
Now, some Spanish soldiers in a phalanx on the right,
So hoist up them halberds in a mass of steel spikes.
We picking three, four heroes, all in history, look a test
Disguise as Columbus, in the front pardner. Yes, I see
Walter Raleigh, up this side friend . . .

(COLUMBUS *and* RALEIGH *leave the crowd.*)

POMPEY

Where this man Mano acquire such knowledge?

MANO

No Horatio Nelson? He ain't in Mass this year? Well, we
going take what we get. Toussaint L'Ouverture and his Haitian rebellion. In front, brother. No Morgan? No Rodney?
Ah, I see George William Gordon. Now I want a test who
could spout the Queen English.

(GORDON *and* TOUSSAINT *join* COLUMBUS *and* RALEIGH.)
Come up here, pardner. Yes, you.
   (*A tall* WARRIOR *appears from crowd.*)
Now I want two masks, tragedy and comedy.
   (*Two* MASKERS *hand over masks to the warrior,*
      which he fixes to a staff.)
As the figure of time and the sea, I giving you these two
masks, and speak the best you could, poetry and all. And
everybody going act, every blest soul going act the history of
this nation. And now, friends and actors, as the sun been on his
road march all day cooling his crack sole in the basin of the
sea, we starting from sunset, through night to the dawn of this
nation. Clear the stage. Darkness, music, and quiet. Right!

   (*All go off. Drum roll and bugle.*)

CHORUS

Before our actors praise his triumph, Time
Shows his twin faces, farce and tragedy;
Before they march with drums and colours by
He sends me, his mace bearer, Memory.
To show the lives of four litigious men,
The rise and ebb of cause and circumstance.
For your delight, I raise them up again,
Not for your judgement, but remembrance.
And now that I revolve his tragic eyes
Upon this stage, I'll show you his device.
This barren height towards which the steps ascend

Is that fixed point round which some issue wheeled.
There our four heroes meet their common end,
There in harsh light, each age must be revealed.
                    (*Steps down.*)
Below them, on this level of the stage,
The spokes of normal action turn their course,
              (*Enter* SPANISH SAILORS.)
Just as these sailors, fished from a drowned age,
Were simple men, obscure, anonymous.
And where the stage achieves its widest arc
The violence of large action shall take place,
Each sphere within the other leaves its mark,
As one man's dying represents the race.
So turn with me, far as your thought will reach,
By this drum's pulse, through the dissolving foam.
        (*Enter to drumbeats,* PRIESTS *and a choir of*
                AMERINDIAN ACOLYTES.)
Time, 1499. A crowded beach.
Columbus leaves on his third voyage home,
Behind him, Governor Bobadilla, whom Isabella, Queen
Of this Castilian colony, has decreed
To charge the old admiral with mismanagement.
By his heart's side, Las Casas, the grey friar.
Santo Domingo, while the sun's lamp descends,
Our actions start, the conqueror cracks the whip
A desolate conch sounds from the waiting ship
These ghosts Time raised are given back their speech.
                    (*Exit.*)

Scene 1

Santo Domingo. 1499. COLUMBUS *sent home in disgrace.*
COLUMBUS; FRANCISCO DE BOBADILLA, *governor*; LAS
CASAS, *bishop of the Indies*; INDIANS, SAILORS,
SOLDIERS, QUADRADO, *officer of the watch.*

LAS CASAS

This is the ship that takes you back to Spain.
Our bodies are ribbed vessels, Admiral,
And being fitted thus, shipwreck is certain
Unless Christ is our pilot.

BOBADILLA

As governor of the province of Santo Domingo,
I accept in the names of our two sovereigns
The resignation of your recent office.
Your Excellency, despite the jurisdiction of our princes,
Saw fit to contradict their majesties' edicts
Against these Indians who are their native subjects,
Against these add, this province's indiscipline,
The mounting, step by step, to your great arrogance
And the mishandling of this Christian conquest.
For this, and all the rest, as public remonstrance,
I have seen it fit to send you home in irons.
I wish you a safe conduct to Cádiz. The chains.

(SOLDIERS *chain* COLUMBUS.)

LAS CASAS

Kneel, for the blessing of the perpetual Church.
Keep in your days that memorable seal
Of Christopher, who bore Christ to the west,
And let this hand that fights for the Indians' cause
Rest heaven's blessing on your foam-white hair.
Jesus et Maria sit nobis in via. God go with you.
(*Exit with* ACOLYTES.)

QUADRADO

Vamos, marineros. Set the ropes free.
Vamos, vamos, the sun is losing light.

(SAILORS *hauling. A sail unfurls.*)

SAILORS

O Dio! Ayuta noy! O que some! Servi soy!
O voleamo! Ben servir O la fede! Mantenir!

(*Drumbeat; exit* BOBADILLA, SOLDIERS, CROWD.)

(*On deck.*)

QUADRADO

Excellency, my captain says the chains need not be used.

COLUMBUS

I'll wear these irons till we fold sail in Spain.
Now lead me to my quarters, my good officer.

QUADRADO (*To* SOLDIER)
You, take the admiral to the captain's quarters.

(COLUMBUS *climbs steps. Exit; a rope ladder let
down from above. Two sailors,* FERNANDO *and*
BARTOLOME, *enter.*)

FERNANDO
A gentle dusk to thee, Quadrado.

BARTOLOME
You took us out of the port most commendably.
Wilt thou have a biscuit, it appears wholesome,
But worms are mining in it, it should suit
Thy opinion of the times.

FERNANDO (*Laughing.*)
He's a poor scholar, Lieutenant,
This world is like an orange, not a biscuit.

QUADRADO
I have forbidden the use of wine till it is issued,
That is well known to you. Give me the wineskin.

GARCÍA
I paid for it.

(*Hands it over.*)

QUADRADO

Some get so drunk they have a sense of justice.

(*Throws away wineskin.*)

When is your watch, Bartolome?

BARTOLOME

With these two Christians. The cemetery patrol.

QUADRADO

See you observe it. Come set the shrouds.

GARCÍA

I hate the bloody authority of that officer.
There's not half a skinful of a man's blood in him.
Didn't he use to drink with us before?

FERNANDO

Come set the shroud, you're a sailor, a drunk one.
He's changed fidelities, but hasn't lost his temper.

BARTOLOME

The penitential officer, he troubles me.
Tonight you'll hear him pace the deck alone.

GARCÍA

The fellow is a lizard, whenever the complexion
Of the world's opinion changes, then so does his.
Since Las Casas, apostle of the Indies, made his sermons,
He has turned into a subtle hypocrite.

FERNANDO (*Fixing ropes.*)
Yet at what cost has this instruction gone?
For every Arawak converted to a Christian
Thousands of them have perished in the mines.
Surely it will be a terribly steep bill
Which these grey friars will present to God.

BARTOLOME
One needs the Indians to work the mines. It's facts.
Either Spain gets the gold, or others will.

GARCÍA
There's an extra wineskin down in the hold. Fetch it.

FERNANDO
Fetch it yourself.

GARCÍA
                           I'll fetch it.
(*Enter* PACO.)
Well, as I live and breathe sour wine, a cannibal.
What dost thou want, little Indian?

PACO
Señor, I seek the officer of the watch.

BARTOLOME
Remove thy cap in the presence of authority.
Didst thou not study the spectacle of the admiral?

GARCÍA

There is thy officer meditating on a biscuit.
Kneel before Lieutenant Fernando and be christened.

FERNANDO

Leave him alone, García, his lip is trembling.

PACO

Señor Officer, I kneel only to God.

GARCÍA (*Grabbing him by the hair.*)
                            Thou art a cannibal,
Thou art a foul mixture, thou wert misbegotten
Between the mailed thighs of a lecherous soldier. Kneel!

PACO

I will kneel down, I will kneel down, my officer.

FERNANDO

García, Quadrado should complete his circuit soon,
If he should find thee torturing the boy . . .

BARTOLOME

You can't talk to this one when he's drunk.

GARCÍA

I'm not the Indian-loving, hypocritical officer.
Swear this as a good Christian. I vow never to eat
White flesh again, be mutinous to a Spanish officer . . .

(*Enter* QUADRADO.)

QUADRADO

Go hang some lanterns up now, all of you. García!

GARCÍA

I am giving this barbarian some instruction.
He flouts all discipline, thanks to your good friars.

BARTOLOME

He's that way when he's drunk, Lieutenant, we had
A few on shore, he don't mean no harm with the kid.
Come, fool, do what the officer has instructed.

FERNANDO

I'll drench his head; he'll be all right, Lieutenant.

GARCÍA

My watch is midnight, and till the appointed glass,
I'll do no other labour for this officer.

QUADRADO

This is the best of the conquest, rebellious trash!

GARCÍA

I won't be called filth before an Indian bastard.

QUADRADO

Bartolome, Fernando, go fetch some lanterns for the admiral.

BARTOLOME

Come, drunkard, let us harvest illuminations.
(*Exit with* GARCÍA.)

QUADRADO

Come, *niño*, we'll walk the pavement of the deck
And watch the sun go down in the dark sea.
What is thy name, why art thou on this vessel?
These rotting ribs that hold the heart of Spain?

PACO

Paco, señor. I am the new *grometto*.

QUADRADO

Thou art a boy of mixed blood. Where is thy father?

PACO

In Spain, my lord, he was a Spanish soldier.
My mother died with the last moon in the mines.
My brothers would not work, and the dogs ate them.

QUADRADO

Of what nation of the Indians art thou?

PACO

Of the Tainos, Excellency.

QUADRADO

The Tainos. Yes, the peaceful ones.

How many will be left to slaughter now?

The Chibchas, the Chocos, the Mayas,

The Lucayos, the Tainos.

PACO

Many of our warriors were killed, señor,

It was a good thing. They were savages.

QUADRADO

Niño, there are no righteous wars. Listen.

(*Takes hourglass.*)

I shall show you the functions of a *grometto*.

This, Paco, is an hourglass, an *ampolleta*.

With each half hour, the top sphere of sand

Dwindles into the lower and marks that time.

Now, when the lower half fills, reverse the glass,

And do this hourly; your watch is at midnight.

Unless we come too early into white seas,

In which event you must steady the glass.

By this we tell our speed and hourly

Express our thanks to Christ for our safe conduct.

Recite for me "The Salve Regina."

PACO

Bendite . . . sea luz, y la Santa Vera Cruz,

Y la Santa Trinidad.

QUADRADO

With less speed and more faith.
What is the matter, what are you watching?

(COLUMBUS *enters above.*)

PACO

The admiral, my officer; why do his own people
Do him this dishonour, what has he done?

QUADRADO

He disobeyed the Queen. Also, he harmed your people.

PACO

Hast thou not killed any savages, my officer?

QUADRADO

Why do you ask?

PACO

My father also was a Spanish soldier.
I remember him, that he was much like you.

QUADRADO

So you have learnt the value of our faith.
            (*Removes a coin.*)
Do you know what this is, my little disciple?

PACO

It is gold, my officer, I have learnt that.

QUADRADO

In the Old World that men called civilization,
Acquire it if you wish to make some mark.
The true stamp of acquisitive man is here,
Compounded in his image, not his maker's.
Study this coin, it gathers darkness around it,
And like the sun, brings its own darkness, guilt.
This barbarous metal, which has less iridescence
Now night descends than the star-crusted sea,
Induced our country, mercenaries, and gentlemen
To sell their souls, for this pus-coloured metal,
Spanish gold.

PACO

It is called money, my officer.
We did not call it that when in the ground.

(GARCÍA *enters unobserved, listening.*)

QUADRADO

We gather this, *grometto*, with much devotion,
As peaceful Indians harvest yellow maize;
It makes our markets and controls the state
And sets up barriers that obscure that view
Where now the admiral achieves his degradation.

PACO

And that is why the admiral looked for these islands?

QUADRADO

You must ask him yourself. Here, keep the coin,
Since my own people taught you of its value,
See how it dims in the bewildering dusk,
But though you take it, please remember this,
That gold outlasts the wearer. Here, keep our God.

PACO

I thank you, my officer, I shall keep it always.

QUADRADO

Also, Paco, until this mutinous vessel reaches Spain,
Think of me not as your officer but as your father.
Now, go fetch the admiral his supper, go.

(*Exit* PACO; *enter* FERNANDO.)

FERNANDO

I have brought the lantern. It will be a rough night.
It will be different for them as cannot sleep.
But I say envy no man anything but his gold.

QUADRADO

Take up the lantern, where's Bartolome?

BARTOLOME *(Singing in hold.)*
There is a fount in Paradise,
A much distasteful place,
So high indeed that fountain jets,
It touches the far lunar sphere.

I can't see a damn in this wet hellhole, move, move.
Here comes the prince of purgatory with his lanterns.

GARCÍA
Be careful with that fire, and plug your bung.

(BARTOLOME *appears.*)

FERNANDO *(Climbing steps to* COLUMBUS.)
I have brought thee a lantern, grizzle gut,
And there'll be food soon for your stomach.
And a sea high enough to quench the stars.

BARTOLOME *(Hanging hammock.)*
O come with me, across the seas,
To where the gold flown is Cathay . . .

What's in that darkened mind of yours, García?

GARCÍA
Gold is the lamp that leads us all to hell.
I saw the remorseful officer, Quadrado,
Give the mestizo a coin, his wealth to the poor.

FERNANDO (*Descends, sets blankets on deck.*)

Well, God rest us all, and wake us for the watch.

Lower the tongue of the lantern, good Bartolome.

BARTOLOME

And God give us all good rest, and spare us envy,

And too much rattling of chains.

FERNANDO

When you pray, friend,

Turn your sour breath away from the wind.

(*They settle.* GARCÍA *lounges on steps, awake.*)

QUADRADO (*Alone*)

Now I am left to walk the deck alone.

The wind is high, the guards are at their poles,

And on this minute, the ship boy should sing out.

BOY'S VOICE

One glass is gone and now the third floweth.

More shall run down, if my God willeth.

QUADRADO

These fellows sleep like brutes without a past.

Murders and theft, they shake them off as horses

Twitch flies from flesh, with a quick shudder.

García, Fernando, and Bartolome. And the admiral.

Only our two remorseful souls are vigilant.
You there on the watch, how is the passage?

LOOKOUT

An open passage, high seas, please God, Lieutenant.

QUADRADO

There are flies on the cordage, flies, flies on these dead.
And when I halt I hear their moans again.

FERNANDO (*Whispering.*)

Bartolome, look, Quadrado . . .

QUADRADO

All of my nights I sweat beads for the slain,
Treading this deck as to a gallows tree.
The frightened moon has scurried into her cave.
The cold quicksilver sweat of fear breaks out
And ghosts creep from the deep slime of the sea.

(MUSIC: *figures of slaughtered Indians emerge
from the shadows.*)

COLUMBUS

Light! Light!

QUADRADO

Who cried out there?
Look, now they come, O Mother of God, prevent them,

As rotten leaves are whirled in a black wind,
I hear the spectres of these slaughtered men
Wail in the wind, the autumn of their race.
One walks there like Sebastian, branched with arrows.
One brings his lantern like a bleeding head.
Mother of God.

(*The ghosts descend through a trapdoor.*)

BARTOLOME

Mother of God, this is most strange, preserve us.

GARCÍA

Get back to sleep. The moon is beautiful.

PACO (*Running up from hold.*)
My officer, my officer, what is it?

QUADRADO

Nothing, nothing. I was at my prayers, a custom
You can put down to nothing and the troubled night.
Is that the admiral's supper? Take it up. Wait!
(GARCÍA *drops back.*)
Did you see nothing as you climbed the steps?

PACO

Nothing but the shadows from the swinging lamp.

QUADRADO

You have not lost the gold I gave you, boy?

PACO

No, my officer, I remember your catechism.

QUADRADO

Remember you have seen nothing, only a soldier
Who cannot sleep, and who has certain fears.
That is the way you will meet your admiral.
I must walk another section of the ship.

(*Exit.* PACO *goes up.*)

PACO

Your supper, Excellency. I have your supper.

COLUMBUS

You are half Indian, why are you on this ship?

PACO

I am a *grometto*, I sing the "Salve" and reverse the glass.

COLUMBUS

I am not very hungry, boy. I am not well.

PACO

Even a god must eat, my admiral.

COLUMBUS

I am not a god, *grometto*.

PACO

Eat, and I will talk out through the night with thee.
(*Pause.*)
Dost thou know of an officer called Quadrado?

COLUMBUS

I knew many officers of several degrees. Why?

PACO

He was a soldier, now he prays for Spain.

COLUMBUS

I am sea-worn, *grometto*, I need some sleep.
There will be many nights ahead of this.

PACO

Weren't thou afraid of the great sea, my admiral?

COLUMBUS

I see that you'll have me talk no matter what.
Well, perhaps it is best, than to remember sins.
Yes, I had great fear, *grometto*, but I had trust.

PACO

Yes, my admiral, in the God who was nailed up.

BARTOLOME (*Below.*)

It's a bad passage. García, go to sleep.

GARCÍA

Be quiet; I'll wake you for the watch.

COLUMBUS

There is a sea the Arabs knew, that scholars called
Mare tenebricosum, the green sea of gloom.
There, pass me the flat plate and I'll show thee, boy.
(*Holds up the plate.*)
Before me, men thought the world's design
Was of this shape, the horizon, the plate's edge,
And on the rim of the world was hell and darkness.
Now, assist me with this iron round my ankles.
This, *niño*, is the certain shape of the world.

PACO (*Kneeling.*)

Tell of the voyage, the monsters, and the lands.

COLUMBUS

And this spoon is Columbus beating on the gates
Of the great princes of the world. A coin,
A coin. I need a coin.

PACO

Here is one, Excellency.

COLUMBUS (*Holds coin.*)

Place this gold here, a circle, like the sun
That daily in its course turns round this iron
And casts its shadow on one side, the night.
The city I was born in, superb Genoa,
Stares with her white breast southward to the sea,
Into the sun, that at its summer solstice
Sets like a burning carrack, fierce with fire,
Behind the pinnacle of Mount Beguia.
Turn up the lantern, and I'll tell thee more.

(PACO *takes down the lantern.*)

I was a weaver's son, strange how we start.
While I worked patiently at my father's shuttle,
I could not guess the web of destinations
That I would weave within the minds of men.

QUADRADO (*Returns.*)

So now he has an Indian for his friend; the boy is safe.

(*Exits.* GARCÍA *creeps up steps.*)

PACO

Señor, now may I have the coin?

COLUMBUS

Thou art shrewd. Thou shouldst go the distance.

GARCÍA (*Below.*)

And the distance being from his purse to my pocket.

PACO

Sit down, señor; sit down, you are not well.

COLUMBUS

A little after sunset, one of my sailors
Noticed the phosphorescence of the sea,
And fishing in the glittering waters found
A twig that had a bunch of withered berries on it.
And there were other signs. The third day passed
And so the dark descended on the sea.
Sometimes it seemed we caught the scent of land.
We waited, quiet, there was silence like this,
There where the shadow of the steady helmsman
Tosses upon the huge screen of the sail.
Merely to breathe seemed an offence to faith.
An hour before the lantern of the moon
Climbed to the stair of heaven where no cloud
Can mantle it, I thought I saw what one might call a light.
I called to my helmsman, Pedro Gutiérrez,
Whose eyes were best in the deceiving darkness.

PACO

What was the light, señor? Were you afraid?

COLUMBUS (*Rises, distracted.*)

Oh, all the cruel patience of the long years,
The fawning humiliation before great princes,

The fears and terrors of the whale-threshed seas
Broke through my cloud now, with his cry of light!

PACO

My admiral, my admiral, sit down, sit down.

COLUMBUS

Honours now hollow are heaped on my crest,
Admiral of ocean, and a tamer of tides,
What will they make of this world is my wonder?
Hypocrites and malefactors have wrecked my work.

PACO
... Excellency ...

COLUMBUS (*Sits.*)

I had hoped to open the green page of this sea
To be a book cartographers could read.
Let me be buried in the backwash of oblivion,
My bones unmarked, my grave a mystery,
And some unlettered sea stone be my tomb.
Yet I held a cross before me, O my Christ,
I did all for God and the lion of Castile,
I did all for God ...

(*He weeps.*)

QUADRADO

I shall get help, my admiral ...

(PACO *descends*, GARCÍA *holds him.*)

GARCÍA

There's gold on you which I need, *grometto,*
So pass it to a Christian who can use it.

PACO

Help, help, my officer.

BARTOLOME

What is it, García? Who cried out?

GARCÍA

Shut your mouth, fool! Look in his shirt for the gold.
He kicks like an animal.

BARTOLOME

Drag him here.

FERNANDO

García, for God's sake, you'll get us all in trouble.

BARTOLOME

Where's the bright coin, little Indian? He bit me.

FERNANDO

That's enough for tonight, in the name of peace. Let go the
Indian, you drunken fool. Look, here's the officer.

QUADRADO (*Enters.*)

What is this, why has the admiral been kept in darkness?

PACO

They tried to kill me for the coin, my officer.

(*He runs over to* QUADRADO, *who draws his sword.*)

GARCÍA

Put up thy trembling sword, *cabrón*,
You can kill nothing but defenceless Indians.
What wilt thou do, kill a good Spaniard?
A normal product of the times, Quadrado?
There, here's new blood for thee.
             (*He squirts wineskin in his eyes.*)

BARTOLOME

Well, sure as Christ, we'll all be hanged now.

GARCÍA

There's no difference in me and this officer.
This is the one the Indians called Carnicero—the butcher.

PACO

Kill him, kill him, my officer.

GARCÍA

Before the affliction of his conscience, this one
Spent all his energies subjugating Indians,

Some by torture, some by terror, some in the mines.
He did some service for the Tainos, too. Quadrado,
You were not called that then, were you, *Teniente*?

PACO

My officer, is this true?

QUADRADO

Give the boy his coin, García.

PACO (*Drawing back from* QUADRADO.)
I want nothing from thee. I know of thee.

FERNANDO

Take it, *niño*, the officer was right.

QUADRADO

I have paid for it, I still pay for it now.
I was called the butcher, but I resign that office.
Others will follow who can learn evil better.
These gestures of affection which I attempt,
The evils I endure from all sorts of men,
This hollow armour of my office, all, *niño*,
I bear because I sought a change of heart.
If this were blood that streamed now from my eyes,
It would not have shook my pity five years ago.
He knows this, and mocks it. I gave the coin
Because I felt I owed thee some affection.
It may be too late.

PACO (*Between* QUADRADO *and* GARCÍA.)
Oh, all of you, all of you,
What must I believe? What must I believe?

QUADRADO
Grometto, do not judge any country by some persons,
Or what its members have done thee; there is only
One race, *grometto*. Man. Go now, observe the glass.

FERNANDO (*To* GARCÍA)
Give the boy the coin, *borracho*, it is his.

GARCÍA
There, *niño*, I return thy wealth to thee,
Come, it is nothing, just a little incident.
What glass is it? There's nothing like some sport
To liven up a long and boring voyage, come.
Recite the glass, *grometto*, the watch is up.

(*All but* PACO *go out.*)

PACO (*Kneeling.*)
One glass is gone, and now the eighth floweth.
More shall run down, as my God willeth.
Good night, my admiral, my captain, *y marineros*.
Buenos noches, Señor Admiral, y maestre, y marineros.
And in the name of Our Father and His son Jesus,
May God grant us a safe passage back to Cádiz.
(*Weeps.*)

(*Blackout.*)

Scene 2

1510. A wharf in Cádiz. Sign: CASA DE LA CONTRACTION.
SAILORS *loading barrels, etc.* WHORES, IDLERS, PACO, *a
few years older, pimping. A* BROKER *and his* NEPHEW
setting up a desk and stool. BARTOLOME, *now a beggar on
crutches, sings:*

BARTOLOME

You generous burghers, Spanish, Portuguese,
Who warm fat, jewelled hands, with winter near,
Here's a poor soldier who sailed the green Indies,
That broke his hulk, that two poor shanks must bear.
He found you empires on seaworthy legs,
But now the winter's coming and he begs.
(*To a* MERCHANT)
A coin, a coin, sir, for an old sailor who sailed with the great,
dead admiral Columbus; who fought, swore, and regrets the
holy wars he fought for an empire.

Ten winters gone he sailed from Cádiz bay.
The admiral cried, "It's young bucks I desire."
India is rich, but not Bartolome.
Now I break wood to fill my winter fire,
For a wise tropic shark removed my legs.
Columbus died, and now his hero begs.

(*To a* BROKER, *as he enters.*)
Oh, sir, sir, it's going to be a biting avengeful autumn, and
I'd hate to use these sticks to keep a tropic fever down.
(SAILOR *rolls barrel near.*) Watch where you roll that
keg, you greed-blinded young bastard! It's Bartolome, the
beggar, señores, once a sailor for her dead majesty Isabella.
(*He goes up to the* BROKER.)

BROKER

There's nothing today, man; besides, you'd drink it.

BARTOLOME

The seed from a sick bull and the spittle from the devil
blind both of you for a pair of furred robbers!

BROKER (*To* NEPHEW)

Now, let that be an example of my preaching.
Tighten your purse strings, invest judiciously.
Now pay attention to the loading sheet, Nephew.
(*Reads.*)
Embarked Cádiz, five sacks sugarcane cuttings,
For the estates in Hispaniola, of Señor Don Fuente,
A snail-cautious settler of accounts. Item:
Crate of Venetian glass, have we checked that?
I can't make out this scholarly scrawl, what the hell is this?

NEPHEW (*Peers.*)

It's your handwriting, Uncle.

BROKER (*Peers.*)

        Slaves, Ashanti. It's my eyes.
That's right, cargo of slaves, Ashanti, thirty.
Transshipment from Cádiz, numbering thirty:
Twenty warriors, one chief, five female, four boys.
Listen, would you prefer to study for the priesthood?
Then pay attention. Paco! Where's García?

PACO

Nowhere on damned wharf, looked inside out.
Went into the bodega, I don't know where he is.
So maybe it's time I get some money?

BROKER

Listen, you get paid when we finished, like the rest.
Where's that García? This cargo is to set out with the tide.

PACO

I know you and your tongue. Damn promises.
Went up and down the wharfs, what you expect me,
Look in the gutters, too? No pay since breakfast.

BROKER

You can work somewhere else if you want, anytime.

PACO

All right, all right, look again.
        (*Exit.*)

NEPHEW

What did he just tell you, Uncle? Who is he?

BROKER

He's from the islands, half cannibal, half Christian,
A pimp and a thief, but otherwise a quick worker.

NEPHEW

How did he get to Spain? What does he do here?

BROKER

Mother of God, would you like me to call him back?
All I know is, he knows the value of cash.

(*Enter* JEW *with belongings.*)

NEPHEW

There's no necessity to be sarcastic, Uncle.

BROKER

I'm sorry I offend you. What is it, señor?

JEW

Pardon me, gentlemen, I am going out to the Indies, and . . .

BROKER

And we, I presume, are directly in your path?

1 5 3

JEW

I was seeking information, but I see you are occupied.
Is it permissible to go aboard the ship?

BROKER (*Brushing the* JEW *aside.*)
And at last, quite drenched, comes the reeking quartermaster.

(*Enter* GARCÍA, *drunk, with* PACO.)

PACO

Señor, before you forget, I bring Señor García.

JEW

I should like some direction, I have papers.
Is this the vessel, the *Cristóbal Colón?*

BROKER

Paco, talk to this gentleman, he is going out to the Indies.
Señor, this one was born there, he will answer questions.
Now, Señor García, if you will sign this list.

JEW

What is that country like, my little friend?

PACO

I carry your bags to the ship right now, señor?

JEW

Is it a place a Jew can live in peace?

PACO

Sure! Las Indias? Fine, plenty sea, sun, green country.
Jew, Tainos, Lucayos, I come from there, beautiful.
Everything fine. You pay me first, señor?

(*The* JEW *pays.*)

GARCÍA

Who's the funny gentleman, Señor Amadeo?

BROKER

Who cares? Are the loading sheets in order?

NEPHEW

He looks to be Jewish, fleeing the persecutions.
The Indian boy, he certainly loves money.

GARCÍA

I thought he was a kike.

JEW (*Apart, praying.*)

O God, rib me with Thy strength
As I embark across the whale-threshed water,
Because my days are swifter than a weaver's shuttle
And are spent without hope.

NEPHEW
What's he saying, Uncle?

BROKER
Remind me to ask him. Now bring them out, García.

PACO (*Returns.*)
Señor Amadeo, I get something to eat now?
Work for you all up and down the damn wharf. Hey, se-
ñor.

BROKER
Can't you wait, boy? Bring them out, García.

PACO (*Draws knife.*)
I know you all the time, long tongue, no cash.
I cut your throat off with this.

(*The* BROKER *pushes him.*)

GARCÍA (*Shouts.*)
Olé, olé, there, Pablo, bring them on for checking.

JEW
My son, do not be vile, and put away the knife.

PACO
He liar, all the time, since before morning, señor.

BROKER

Oh shut up, and get out of the way if you can't wait.

(*A cargo of* SLAVES, *chained, brought on.*)

JEW

What are these people?

BROKER (*Wryly*)

They will be travelling with you, Excellency.

JEW (*Softly*)

The stranger that dwelleth with you, saith the prophet,
Shall be unto you as one born among you,
And thou shalt love him as thyself.

BROKER

Amen, amen, Abraham.

GARCÍA

Provided he splitteth not the profits too unfairly.
Come on now, line them up there, Amadeo.
Not a bad bunch, where did you get those from?

BROKER

You know they sell each other after their battles.
Look at this one, though, he is some sort of king.
Notice the excellent quality of his sweat, taste it.
And those sinews, I've put him down at three pieces.

GARCÍA

But this one, sickly, little. Look at those teeth.
But he has some spirit. What is this one, a scholar?
These the King's sons? You can throw them in as extra.

(*They examine* SLAVES.)

BROKER

I can't throw in anything extra, I can't afford it.

GARCÍA

What's the King's name?

NEPHEW (*Checking.*)
Mano.

GARCÍA

They haven't been branded yet?

BROKER

I don't want to brand them here.

GARCÍA

I think I have an iron on board. All right, move them on.
I'll separate them when we get aboard.

(*The* SLAVES *are loaded aboard.*)

BROKER

You're a hard-bargaining bastard, García.

GARCÍA

I got a sick mother.

(*The* BROKER *pays* GARCÍA.)

NEPHEW (*To the* JEW)

You may go aboard now, señor, and a safe passage.
It is a long voyage, I hope you can endure it.

JEW

That is kind of you, I wish you the same.
Good night, good night, my little friend.

PACO

Sometimes I wish to go back there myself, the Indies.
But I have bad memories. They say half of my people
Are left, and those are dying. *Adiós*, señor.

(*The* JEW *goes aboard.*)

BROKER

Do me a favour once you take charge, García,
Don't treat them like humans, they're more valuable . . .

GARCÍA (*Ascends steps.*)

I'll treat them like my sick mother. *Adiós*, Amadeo.

BROKER

Adiós.

GARCÍA (*Throws coin to* PACO.)
Look after the girls for me, it's a long trip.
Ah, where's Quadrado now, eh? And his catechism?
(*Climbs the steps.*)
Where did you get that nephew from?

BROKER (*Shouting to ship.*)
It's his first day here, he's my sister's son.
He should be in a monastery, he's very profound.
(*A* MERCHANT *passes.*)
How is it, friend, did you ship anything?

MERCHANT
One of my ships, that by some ill luck steered
Out of its course from the Canaries this last week,
Ran up against some pirates, Dutch or English.
They say the numbers are increasing, and I know
There's more of the buzzards hanging on the horizon
And waiting for the fat cargoes to pass by them.
What did you ship today?

NEPHEW (*Checking.*)
Thirty or so Negroes . . .

BROKER (*Hurriedly*)
A few, most of them sickly.

MERCHANT

Troubles, that's all a man inherits, troubles.
I hope nothing happens to your shipment, Señor Amadeo.
I have had bad luck. I'll tell you where the profits
Are multiplying now. I have a cousin who's an armourer,
And you should see the trade he gets; it's certain
That with this piracy, which the King must resent,
And with this struggle for the possession of the Indies,
There's a war coming with the English, that's where the
    money is.
The sea is an ungrateful business.

BROKER
           I know, I know.

(*Exit* MERCHANT.)

PACO

Hey, señor, how about my money?

BROKER

Here you are, Paco, is that enough?
(*He throws coins.* PACO *and* BARTOLOME *scramble for them.*)
Come, my profound accountant, take up the furniture.

(*Exit* BROKER *and* NEPHEW.)

PACO

Why don't you work another wharf, Bartolome?

BARTOLOME
                      Well, half of it, friend, half,
Or would you have me clout you with this crutch?
We're both victims of civilisation, little savage.

PACO
Go pick up garbage, you sickness.
I earned this fairly, I did work for it,
I'm not a bad singer of vile songs.

WOMAN (*Calling offstage from tavern.*)
Paco, *¡hola!*, Paco. Where's the little savage? Paco, come
   here.
      (*She enters, followed by* SOLDIERS *and* WHORES.)
Inside, *grometto*, or sing us a holy song.

PACO
For money? Then listen. "The Song of Conversion."
              (*Sings.*)

I linger on the darkened pier when the great ships have gone
And curse the Spanish admiral called Cristóbal Colón.
I think of catechisms the grey friars made us learn,
How if I was no Christian child in what great fires I'd burn.
And now that I'm in holy Spain the Church may shut its
   doors,
For we're dancing to the fiddles and
The laughter of the whores.

WHORES

Dance, dance, we made some money today!

PACO

The friars in the Indies said that men live differently.
I had not met the merchants with their special piety.
I cannot doubt the friars' truth, but I have bread to earn,
And anyhow, the Inquisition makes the Jews to burn,
So I left my pagan paradise for civilisation's shores,
And now you know the difference 'tween
Unjust and righteous wars.

(*Music and dancing.*)

BARTOLOME

The sailors and the conquerors do homage to a queen
And many a Spanish regiment is rotting on the green.
It takes a hundred niggers now to dig the gold we earn,
And I'm too dumb to understand investment and return,
So keep the jewels in the vaults, and pity out-of-doors,
While we'll dance to the fiddles and
The laughter of the whores.

(*Laughter. Drums beat off.*)

FIRST WHORE

It's more soldiers, there's a ship in the harbour.
There's war in the air, friend.

SECOND WHORE

> And tough times ahead for us.

PACO

Who are they going to fight? I have seen many soldiers.

FIRST WHORE

They're preparing many years now against the English,
And they have made expeditions against the Dutch.
I lost two brothers who fought against the Dutch.
This King is preparing a great Armada.

PACO

Does a Spanish soldier live well now? How are they paid?

SECOND WHORE

Well, you are fed and clothed, some of the mercenaries
Can do well, and there is no faith asked of them
While they are paid. Oh, I love the thought of war.

(*The* SOLDIERS *take leave of the* WHORES *and run off.*)

BARTOLOME

Well, it's a better life if a man had both legs
Than scrounging on the piers, begging from merchants.
They're out to conquer England and preserve the Indies.
If I had half of my strength, that's where I'd be.

(*Drums sound nearer.*)

PACO

Oh, the drums, the drums, colours and the fifes.
My father's profession calls me. Bartolome, here's a coin.
I'm on the side with the money still, Quadrado!
And I leave you this kingdom of the wharf, *adiós, adiós!*
(*He runs off.*)

BARTOLOME

Come on, let's go into the inn where the drinks are warm.
It seems to me I felt there the edge of the winter.
(*Sings.*)
For a wise tropic shark removed his legs,
And now the winter's coming, and he begs.
(*Exit, limping, after* WHORES. *Martial music.*)

(*Fade-out.*)

Scene 3

Aboard ship. Near dawn. Two SPANISH SAILORS *dicing. In
the hold below* SLAVES *chanting.*

FIRST SAILOR

Christ! You've got all the luck in this world.

SECOND SAILOR

I'm a good Spaniard. How about another throw? For
daybreak?

FIRST SAILOR

What's the bet? That the sun won't rise?

(*Rises.*)

I'd better take a look below the decks.

Sometimes the sick ones kill themselves.

SECOND SAILOR

Not your responsibility. How can you stand the stench?

FIRST SAILOR

Well, for God's sake, don't wave the lantern about.

We're in warm seas, and nearing the islands,

And there's Dutch and English privateers about.

Pass me the lantern.

SECOND SAILOR

Hey! You can't leave me in the dark!

FIRST SAILOR

Dawn is enough to count your profits by.

(*He moves off with lantern.*)

SECOND SAILOR

Pity you have no luck, amigo.

FIRST SAILOR

I don't believe in luck. I believe in God.

SECOND SAILOR

It's just faith. Faith in the dice, amigo.

FIRST SAILOR

Sure, sure. Your father must have been at the foot of the
cross.

(*Exit. The* JEW *enters above.*)

JEW

Because they have wrenched my people from the roots,
I am like a shattered timber cast adrift. O God,
The shores of the new lands will soon be known.
Preserve my faith, O Lord, comfort Thy people.
(*He exits.*)

Scene 4

The ship: SLAVES, *men and women and two children,
chained in pairs, emerge from hold. The sick* KING *attended
by* WOMEN.

MALE SLAVE

Look, though we do not wish it, dawn will break.

WOMAN SLAVE

We cannot stop the law of time: only the gods.

MALE SLAVE

My gods and yours are different. I am an Ibo.

WOMAN SLAVE

Were you captured in the battle with our tribe?

MALE SLAVE (*Laughs.*)

I was forced to fight, but I am no warrior.
It is comical, I was captured during the confusion.
But as you say it is nothing. Your King is quiet.

WOMAN SLAVE

I do not think that he will last the long voyage.
He lost his pride in his battle against the Ibo.
I lost two sons when you attacked our village.
My husband is somewhere with the rest, in there.

MALE SLAVE

I think that the fellow chained to me is dead.
Can you help me lug him onto the deck?

WOMAN SLAVE

Why should I touch the dead? The dead are lucky,
They have caught the happy plague.
Oh God, my sons.

MALE SLAVE

Day will break soon, and we are nearing islands,
I can hear the creaking of seabirds this morning.

(*Pause.*)

We can see his face when the dawn comes up.

WOMAN SLAVE

You are a funny one. Why do you wish to see it?

MALE SLAVE

He must have died last night. Are you afraid?

WOMAN SLAVE

Man is a beast. Man is a beast. Believe me.

MALE SLAVE

It is true, I have never understood fighting.

I had a small place, near a river, fishing,

And I had no enemies, I was waiting for a wife.

WOMAN SLAVE

Yes, bring children into the world, to bury them.

MALE SLAVE

It is how the gods made it. We must bear that.

WOMAN SLAVE

Explain it.

MALE SLAVE

You women have it hard, daylight is here.

WOMAN SLAVE

Oh, look at his face, oh God.

MALE SLAVE

Why, do you know him?

WOMAN SLAVE

Yes, it is my husband.

MALE SLAVE

Your husband?

WOMAN SLAVE

He used to praise all war as honourable,
And boasting always of the beauty of death,
Look at him now, in his beauty of death.

MALE SLAVE

I never had children.

WOMAN SLAVE

I am not thinking of warriors but their women.
This is the kind of suffering I would have honoured,
Oh God, oh God, what will happen to my sons?

MALE SLAVE

Be patient. Life is very long.

WOMAN SLAVE

Africa, Guinea.

(*She weeps.*)

MALE SLAVE

Life is good, woman.

WOMAN SLAVE

Africa, the white birds by the river's edge at sunrise,
The clear waters over white stones, the children
Splashing in mud.

(*They begin a new chant.*)

MALE SLAVE

It is strange what the gods allow. Listen,
Your people are singing. The children are frightened.

WOMAN SLAVE

Do they whip them, too?

(*A* CHILD *comes over.*)

MALE SLAVE

I do not know.

Is this one of the King's sons?

WOMAN SLAVE

Yes. Man is a beast. Man is a beast.
What will they do this one, at such an age?

MALE SLAVE

They will put the mark on him, as we do beasts.

(*Pause, chanting.*)

In our country, we thank the gods for each day.

WOMAN SLAVE

And so do we. I suppose so do all lucky men.

MALE SLAVE

I do not believe in luck. I believe in God.

Here comes our days-long anguish, let us be brave.

(GARCÍA, *whip in hand, appears.*)

GARCÍA

All right, stir them up there, get them awake.

We'll get them dancing to limber up their muscles,

They must land in a purchasable condition.

How many dead this voyage?

SAILOR

There's one dead here.

GARCÍA

That one wasn't worth much anyway.

Pablo, get the drum and start their exercises.

You, take the carcass below, do you hear me?

Get below, you bastard, d'you understand?

(*He kicks a* SLAVE. *Drumming starts; no one moves.*)

I hate to use this, but you'd better start moving.
What's the matter, doesn't the King love music?
Come on, everybody's equal here, Your Majesty.
  (*They start to move slowly, wearily; the* KING *falls.*)
Wait a minute, stop the drumming, stop it.
Get up, Your Majesty, get up and dance.
Take that child away from him. Now, come on, dance.
      (*The* KING *is unable to move.*)
He's a stubborn bastard.

SAILOR

This might help him.

  (*He punches the* KING, *who falls; the* SLAVES *stop.*)

GARCÍA

Keep them dancing and drag the body off.
Keep the child from him. Come, tear him off.

(*The* CHILD *is lifted off the* KING's *body and thrown near
the steps.*)

JEW (*Coming down the steps.*)
Señor, the child, I will buy the boy from you.

GARCÍA

Get out of the way, this is none of your concern.
      (*To* PABLO, *another sailor*)
You're fumbling up everything, keep them dancing.

JEW

The boy. The child. I'll buy him from you.

GARCÍA

I can't hear you. You want to buy the boy?

JEW

Yes, yes, how much?

GARCÍA

Twenty pieces.

JEW

I have only fifteen; will you take fifteen?

GARCÍA

Seventeen. Two more when we land. Fifteen right now.
All right, enough. Take them below and feed them.
Fifteen all right with you, he's a king's son?
Let me tell you, you're a damned fool, mister.
The boy is sure to die of one thing or another.

JEW

Not if I own him. Come, come to me, child.

(*The* CHILD *huddles to him.*)

SAILOR (*Aloft.*)

Sail, sail to leeward.

GARCÍA

What colours, you idiot?

SAILOR

Inglesi, Inglesi.

(*The* SLAVES *herded out through the central door, back. The
door is closed. Chanting offstage more urgent now, wails
and screams from the* WOMEN.)

GARCÍA

Tell them there's no gold aboard, only niggers.
(*To* JEW)
Get out of the way, sir, with your purchase.
Get out the cannon there, stand by to fire.
(*Cannon fire.* MALE SLAVE *comes up through the trapdoor,
stabs* GARCÍA.)
O Mother of God, get me a priest, I am dying.
(*He falls.*)
When did I offend you, Jew?

JEW (*Bending over* GARCÍA.)
It was the slave, I could not kill a man. You killed the King.

GARCÍA

The darkness comes, O Mother of God.
Do not leave me alone, sir.

(*Cannon fire.*)

JEW

. . . I have to save the boy.

What is it?

GARCÍA

I remember Quadrado . . . Oh God . . . Life has gone the
dial.

(*He dies.*)

JEW (*With* CHILD.)

That is a passage you must go alone, poor man.
Come stand by me; perhaps we shall be taken,
But we shall find roots in the new land together.
Come, move out of this danger of the battle.
I will take care of thee, as my own son,
For we are outcasts together in one sorrow.

(*Blackout.*)

(*Cannon fire. Music.*)

Scene 5
Boyhood of Raleigh

Music: Reprise of PACO'S *song. A wintry beach in England.*
PACO, *an old beggar, walking.*

PACO (*Singing* BARTOLOME'S *song.*)
You generous burghers, English, Portuguese,
Who warm white jewelled hands, with winter near.
Here is old Paco, who sailed the green Indies.
The winter wind blows round his tattered legs . . .

A man may walk on all the broken beaches of this world, and come to the warmth of an inn in winter, and *sí*, death is the landlord. I've seen the four-hued seasons, the fox-coloured autumn, the broad-leafed summer, and the green spring, but I'll be damned if I can get used to this English winter; it moulders an old man's flesh. My purse, where's my purse? The fur from this old Flemish collar's gone, and my old teeth ache. I need new boots. There's enough wreckage here to start a fire with. It's cold, winter's coming on like the great grey wolf, and me with no summer in these swollen veins. Wait, here's something half hidden in the sand. (*Finds stumps of wood.*) Nothing, only wood. Still, it will make a fire. Count the coins again, count the purse. Here's five Spanish pieces, two Dutch, and God knows where I lost Quadrado's coin these last forty years.

(BOYS' *voices off.*)

Put the coins away, they're after you. The little dogs are hounding the old bear.

(*Enter young* RALEIGH *and young* GILBERT.)

RALEIGH (*Dancing around him.*)
It's the old Spaniard, Paco, Paco, ay, cannibal!

PACO

Keep from me, you two, I chew human flesh.

GILBERT

Leave him, Walter, he hates to be annoyed.

PACO

That's right, you tell him, *niño*, I chew English flesh.
You come near old Paco the cannibal and see.
I'll split your heads open with this bit of wood.

RALEIGH

Look at his eyes and his hair. Throw it, Spaniard.

PACO

You're a brave imp. What's your name, boy?

RALEIGH

What're you doing on this beach?

PACO

What's your friend's name, then?

GILBERT

He's Walter Raleigh. I'm his cousin Humphrey Gilbert.

PACO

Well then, Master Gilbert, if you're a Christian,
Tell your friend here, I'm a great chewer of children.
My people, the Tainos, were great eaters of Christians.
But you're grand gentlemen's sons, I can see,
So throw a coin to an ancient sailor, for honestly,
I have no sides but the sharp wind finds holes
Through the ribs of this wreck I am, friends.
Do that, and I'll be off.

GILBERT

Are you cold, sir?

PACO

Ay, ay, boy, cold in three languages.

RALEIGH

I've heard of him, cousin, he's a great liar.
He tells lies in all the inns, for drink,
And he's a foul old Spaniard.

PACO

Half, half, mate.
The rest of this carcass is proud Indian, Tainos.
(*Hopping around.*)
Oh, it's the biting cold I can't shake off by dancing.
But a coin or two from you Christian boys, I'll tell you.
You've heard tell of the great Admiral Columbus.

I fed the old man his supper once, you doubt it?
Then leave me alone!

(*He hurls wood.*)

GILBERT

Shall I give him a coin, cousin?

PACO

Look, do you see this wood I threw at you?
Bring it here, mate, and I'll tell you a thing.

GILBERT

Here.

(*He throws a coin.*)

PACO

Thank you, lad. It's a fragment of Spanish ship.
Can you read what's marked on it, Master Gilbert?

RALEIGH

Don't go near him, cousin.

PACO (*To* RALEIGH)

There, you read it, then, though there's sea grime
Grooved in the letters; can you read it, then?

RALEIGH (*Spelling out letters.*)

El Dorado, El Dorado.

PACO

Ah! El Dorado, now, have you heard of that?

RALEIGH

Yes, it's in the west, but it's a Spanish legend.

PACO

Legend, legend, he says, like a sceptical Christian.
I was like you, my boy, before I saw the great legend
That Quadrado called Europe; but now what would you say
If I said, kissing this cross, that I've seen the legend.
Would that provoke a coin from your purse, lad?
(*He pauses.*)
This El Dorado is a golden country,
I showed it once to an officer called Quadrado.
Oh, I've tossed like an old cork on the seas of the world.
Seen whales and marvels in my old age, but this,
This bewilders belief. This bit of log, mates,
Tells of a golden city in the green heart of Guiana,
And these two words, they mean the gilded king.
But it'll take another coin to unlock my tongue.

RALEIGH

Then if this legend is so certain,
Why haven't the Spanish found the city, sir?

(*They draw near him.*)

PACO (*Sits.*)

Because out of the deep beliefs of their religion
The cunning Indians kept the secret from them,
For the Spanish, you know, destroyed my people.
There's many Spanish expeditions looked for it.
They're rusting in the emerald jungles now.
It's a far voyage.

RALEIGH

How far is it, old man?

PACO

Far as I am from home, and the warm islands.
It's a perilous voyage, farther than Columbus,
And farther than the great conquistadors have found,
Men of the stamp of Cortés and Quesada.
Resilient men, formed in the Spanish temper,
Who conquered Mexico and Montezuma,
But this gold legend on this worm-riddled wood
They'll never find.

GILBERT

The English will.

PACO

Well, when you do, remember your old friend Paco.
Look, mates, I'll tell you a dying secret, but
Would your cousin lend me the price of a jug?

GILBERT

Give him a coin, cousin. Now, will you show us where?

(RALEIGH *complies.*)

PACO (*Drawing on the sand.*)

Thanks, little Christian. Well, this here's the whale's bath,
The great Atlantic, where a great city drowned.
Here's a dead wealth of yellow weed, Sargasso,
And these moss-covered pebbles at my old boots,
These are the emeralds which Columbus christened
Salvador, Cuba, Jamaica, Hispaniola,
Innumerable islands, then the Isle of Trinity,
And there, among the tangle of this seaweed,
Where I put down a gold coin in its tangle,
There is the city of Manoa, El Dorado.
(*He starts, leaps back.*)
Do you hear the barking of dogs? They're hunting me.
They hunted us with dogs once. Go back from me.
There's a wolf's cry on the wind, they're coming.

GILBERT

There are no wolves in this country. Do you fear dogs?

PACO

I've seen them tear men to pieces, all my flesh,
For gold. Christian dogs besides. Go back from me.

RALEIGH (*Drawing* GILBERT *aside.*)

He is mad, cousin. Are you sick, sir?

PACO

Dying on two worn feet, son, weary from walking
Thousands of miles, all over the map of Europe.
Tamoussi, Tamoussi, my own gods call me back.
(*Staring wildly.*)
Would you do me a favour in return, my sons?

GILBERT

So, you frighten us.

RALEIGH

So, we'll do what you ask us, if we can.

PACO

There is an old wisdom which my tribe possessed.
To tell the season of their coming death, the Tainos,
By some scent in the wind, the altering of a feather,
Or the warm scent of the autumn-coloured fox.
This wind carries the stench of rotting flesh.

GILBERT

It's nothing but the old smell of the sea.

PACO

It is the sea that separates me from my gods,
And brought destruction to my simple people.
Come, do you know some high place in this country?
And leave me there, before the first snow comes?

RALEIGH

I know a height, barren with sea rocks, where
You can sit quietly and watch the sinking west;
There's nothing there.

(PACO *removes a crucifix.*)

PACO

Then take the crucifix and the coins I gathered,
And lead me to it, for the time of the dog is here.

RALEIGH

If you look there, then climb the cleft in the rocks,
It winds its narrow path up from the sea.
There you shall find a place just as you wished.
(*He leads* PACO *to the steps.*)

PACO

Is it there? Yes, I think I see the track.
And so it goes, whatever track we take
It leads us all to the cold height of death.
I have strength enough to climb to it alone,
That is the fashion in which my people die.
Go, go back. I hear the wolf howling again.
If you go to Manoa, death will find you there.
Good night, you Christian boys, Paco is gone.

RALEIGH

Come, cousin, and take up the fragment of the vessel.

(*They go off reluctantly.*)

PACO (*Climbing.*)

So the grey wolf of death trots after me.
O Quadrado, in all this I have learnt nothing.

(*Exit. Blackout.*)

(*The* CHORUS *enters.*)

CHORUS

Those ribs which bulwarked Spain's imperial pride
Lie wrecked and bone-white down the English coast,
Wrenched by ungovernable winds that scattered wide
Ships, masts, and soldiers, which the Armada cost.
After twelve years' imprisonment in the Tower,
With two great factions at an unstable peace,
The Stuart monarch, England's James the First,
Grants Walter Raleigh conditional release
To find that fable, turreted with gold
That, like a coin, gathers the dark around it.
It is 1617 now, Guiana, night.
(*Lute music softly.*)
Stillness, a lonely lute plucks at the nerves.
The idling lanterns with their yellow light
Gild every mind from captain to mere sailor,

And now we peer into the unmapped night
Whose stars ride quietly from the anchored fleet,
The ships: the *Jason*, under Captain John Pennington;
The *Confidence*, Commander, Captain Wallastons;
The *Flying Hart*, Commander, Sir John Ferne;
The *Golden Fleece*, the ship of war; *Corentyne*,
Under Commander Captain Laurence Keymis;
The *Destiny*, under Sir Walter Raleigh.

(Exit.)

Scene 6

1617. The search for El Dorado. The deck of the Destiny.
Enter RALEIGH *and* KEYMIS.

RALEIGH

I have sent for you particularly, Captain Keymis,
Not only as my officer but a friend,
To tell you my decision concerning tomorrow.

KEYMIS

I can guess it.

RALEIGH

Come to the rail, Laurence, and try to think my thoughts.
For a good friend, here, let me lean on your shoulder;
A good friend's mind should be chameleon-like
And take its colours from opposite affections.

KEYMIS

I find that somewhat parasitical, Sir Walter.

RALEIGH

Imagine yourself placed in my own position,
Beyond these fireflies of the anchored fleet.
You can discern the black leaves of a forest,
So far translated into no civilized tongue.
So once another admiral years ago
Saw a prone country, still with its maidenhead,
The virgin sea, through which no prow had entered,
And sealed its nuptials in the name of Spain.
Like me, his own impetuous, rebellious nature
Offended monarchs; he died disdained, obscurely.
Above my own head hangs a thirsty axe;
The King, with his limp and lily-sinewed wrist,
Can write my vein out, with a flick of the pen.

(*He starts down the steps, followed by* KEYMIS.)

KEYMIS

The King is more concerned with bargaining with the
    Spaniard
Than with your nature; you are of a breed, sir,
Against his policy. Who's left in England now?
The admirals, earls, and boisterous captains
Who shivered all the strength of Spain, her provinces,
They are buried now, some in strange parts of the sea.

RALEIGH

And do you know by what he weighs us? Gold.
He spared me for that purpose. What time is it?

KEYMIS (*Moving towards table.*)
It must be almost eight o'clock. And so I take it,
Since we have burnt the town at Trinidad,
An act that certainly should incense the King,
And since we stand outside Guiana, full of doubts,
That tomorrow we attack the fort at San Thome?

RALEIGH

We must not fail this time to find Manoa.
I want my son to come with us tomorrow, Keymis.
I feel a dewy sweat, I have caught the fever.
If I should be too weak to go, you will command.
But it should pass. First let us study the map.

(KEYMIS *unrolls a map on the table.*)

KEYMIS

It's not changed much since the last time, my lord.

RALEIGH

Wait.

(*Pause.*)

KEYMIS

What is it, Sir Walter?

RALEIGH

No. As I stood here and you unrolled the map,
With my life in the balances tomorrow,
I remembered my boyhood and an old dim sailor,
An old man with two worlds mixed in his blood,
And a strange prophecy which he made to me.
How sovereign death controls Guiana's green,
And that my voyages there would bring me death.
      (*Enter* RALEIGH'S SON, *unobserved, with a lute.*)
I saw in my condition of this giddy fever
How the sea's jaws swallowed Sir Humphrey Gilbert,
And bones of Spanish conquerors mixed with vines.

SON

Think of your reputation, Father.

RALEIGH (*Turns.*)

Welcome. I heard you on the lute.
      (*To* KEYMIS)
Some days my mind is clear and crystal green,
And perfect as a summer of the sea, and then
A cloud of my uncertainty mantles it.

SON

It's nothing but the fever, Father.

RALEIGH

Yes, but the gilding fever known as greed.
Come, study the map, boy, you go with Captain Keymis.
When I am absent, consider him your father.

KEYMIS (*Showing* RALEIGH'S SON.)

This lake here is the Rupununi, lying between
The river Essequibo and the Rio Branco.
There is Canelos, a land of cinnamon trees.
These are the tributaries which I charted,
And this is the fort which we assault tomorrow.
We are sure our prisoner, Governor de Berrio,
Knows something of the site of this great city.

    (*The clock strikes eight.*)

It has struck eight, shall I bring in the governor?

RALEIGH

Yes, bring in the hypocrite.

    (*Exit* KEYMIS.)

You see the sad trade of conquest, study it well.

SON

       Father, are you afraid?

RALEIGH

I feel so hollow, boy. Yes, I am afraid,
But for you, too; long memories disturb me.
Know that I would not give your life, my son,
For a roomful of all the jewels in Manoa.

SON

Why should I die, my lord? Am I a bad soldier?

RALEIGH

No, you do well, you do well. And here's the governor.

(*Enter* BERRIO, KEYMIS.)

Señor de Berrio, my son who carries my name;

My friend and captain Laurence Keymis.

Be seated, sir, and have some Spanish wine.

BERRIO

Gracias.

(*He sits.*)

RALEIGH (*Pacing.*)

Excellency, we will get down to business straight.

Your Excellency has for some years been governor of
   Trinidad,

Which is the door and gateway to the west.

It is my confirmed impression, contradict me,

That despite the pressing duties of your office

On occasions you have conducted expeditions

To find the legend that hides in the darkness there.

BERRIO (*Smiles.*)

This is good Spanish claret, Señor Admiral.

RALEIGH

Do you recall a Captain Whiddon, Excellency?

BERRIO

Yes, I know this English soldier Whiddon.

I also know our countries are at peace,

And that he broke our compact; that English ships
Attack our provinces in these islands, against the peace.
Yes, I know Whiddon, and why you ask me that,
To explain your sacking of the town of San José
And justify the death of my own nephew.

RALEIGH

Perhaps Your Excellency might find it awkward
To recall your treacherous—pardon me—surprising
Entertainment of this English officer.

BERRIO (*Rises.*)

Is this why I am brought before Your Excellency?
To exchange memoirs? A week ago my men were
    massacred,
The city I administered sacked and burnt.

RALEIGH

Much like your treatment of the Indians, señor.

BERRIO (*Sits.*)

We all did it once. Now they do it with Negroes.
Unfortunately, that is how one starts an empire.

RALEIGH

You still consider Spain a power, señor?

BERRIO

There is no Spain here now.
It is a different thing to Europe, these are the Indies,
With a different climate and a policy that must change.
I think that despite Whiddon, whose death I sanctioned,
That I was compensated, as you might say, enough.
All that I built was burnt. We are at peace.

RALEIGH

Perhaps. But then why should I savour of an ass,
With your honourable Spanish army at my back,
When I must force my passage through Guiana?

BERRIO

Why must, señor?

RALEIGH

What?

BERRIO

Why must you pursue this fable of Guiana?
Will that not mean a slaughtering of Indians?

RALEIGH (*Shouts.*)
I am not a Spaniard, man.

KEYMIS

Sir Walter.

BERRIO (*Rising.*)

No, I am a Spaniard and responsible to my country.

And, you are English, your star in the ascendant.

But to me you are a finished phenomenon, my friend,

In that this pursuit of wealth, of personal glory,

Is of a finished age, the age of conquest, cruelty.

The gold is veining out.

KEYMIS

Is that why you preach?

BERRIO

As governor I pursued my Catholic precepts,

Brought here by our first admiral and Las Casas,

That what men take away out of a country

They must restore by something else.

Our mines are finishing, and the more profitable pursuits

Of growing cities, establishing Christian culture,

Is now the general concern, not avarice.

The individual reputation must be dimmed,

For the establishment of commerce, justice.

I am the proconsul of a new empire, señor.

KEYMIS

Now will Your Excellency look at this map?

RALEIGH (*To* BERRIO)

You tell me not to pursue my search for El Dorado.

Must I presume, before the discoveries,

Before Cortés, Pizarro, Bilbão, Alcázar
There was no Montezuma, nor Peru; in fact no gold.
No massacre of natives, no Spanish imperialism
Under you Christian conquerors? Let us be honest.
I'm ageing. I believe in the existence of this city,
And so do you, I know, and Keymis, but you,
Exhibiting that familiar Spanish arrogance . . .

BERRIO

Señor, I am too tired to bear arrogance.
(*Rises.*)

RALEIGH (*Enraged*)
If you please!
Think all the world the property of Spain.
But Spain is shattered, her wealth will be ours,
I am not an even-tempered man, señor.

SON

Father, there is no need to be so angry with him.

RALEIGH (*Turning on* SON.)
I am your admiral, not your father now.

(*Pause.*)

KEYMIS

Señor Berrio, do you recognise certain names here?

BERRIO (*Amused*)

I see a map whose drawings are as haphazard
As any I have done concerning this fable.

KEYMIS

And where is the best direction to this fable?

BERRIO

I have a fatal statement for you gentlemen.

RALEIGH

Which is?

(*He sits.*)

BERRIO

There is no El Dorado.
There is a story devised for malice by the Indians.
It is a vicious fable, it is like Atlantis, it is like
Columbus's Cipango, like your own John Mandeville.
The more you pierce Guiana and explore it,
Pages of pages part before you, volumes of forest;
But El Dorado has no meaning, there are the bones
Of ruined Spanish expeditions, and nothing else.

KEYMIS

Yet you yourself have made cynical expeditions
Of this nature.

BERRIO

That is why I speak.

I cannot warn you of the terrible expense

When men or nations turn to beasts for gold.

RALEIGH (*Rises angrily.*)

Very well then, to be considered a beast!

Issue this order to the captains, Keymis.

Despite the orders of the King of England,

Despite the hypocrisy of this cunning Spaniard,

Raleigh now risks his life, his soldiers' lives,

His son's, and all the weight, experience

Of his life, to find this fool's gold and be King of it!

Burn down the Spanish fort and find Manoa,

And now, señor, I wish you a good night.

(*He exits.*)

KEYMIS

I have not seen him so angry for some time.

He has a tongue that wounds his friends.

BERRIO

He is a sensitive but a dangerous man.

If he is your friend, then I say, look again.

He uses people.

KEYMIS

And you know nothing?

BERRIO

Oh, you persistent English, I know nothing.
I should like some rest. I wish him luck.
But I know this will bring some terrible price.

SON

My father is no coward, Señor de Berrio.

BERRIO

Sí, niño. No coward. But a frightened man. Good night.

(*Exit* BERRIO, KEYMIS.)

SON (*Picks up lute and sings.*)
Gather ye money while ye may,
Old Time is still a-flying,
And that same price you raised today
Tomorrow will be dying.
That yellow coin of heaven, the sun,
The higher he's a-getting.
Pursue him still and you may run
A profit ere his setting.
So be you wise and be you bold
But let this keep you bonny.
Joy is a thing that's bought and sold.
So sing hey money, money.

(RALEIGH, *cloaked, enters above, listens to*
end of song, and descends.)

RALEIGH

Go, get to bed, boy, there's soldier's work at sunrise.
Excuse my anger. Know I love you. Now get to bed.

SON

How is your fever? You should rest, Father.

RALEIGH

I have the fever and I cannot rest,
I think of my responsibility, and each man's life,
Of your sweet mother, of how greed makes men mad,
And that dull ache of absence called a wife.

(*Lights fade as* RALEIGH *exits. Slow drumbeats start.*
Trumpet calls. To suggest passage of time—spot on
CHORUS *at left and spot on* RALEIGH *motionless.*
Enter CHORUS.)

CHORUS

The lanterns of the fleet die one by one,
The wandering moon rides through a foam of clouds,
As Raleigh walks the deadened deck alone.
The false grey of daylight fills the east.
He waits with a few soldiers, alone, aboard,
(*Spot on* RALEIGH.)
Through morning to the dead dial of noon.
The hours pass, till a far drum is heard.

(*Lights up slowly.*)

SAILOR

Smoke, sir! It's the fort, they've burnt the fort.

RALEIGH (*Wearily*)

And that drum's pulse means failure and defeat.
Lower the longboat there for Captain Keymis.
Can you shout what you see there, fellow?

SAILOR

Aye, aye, sir. It's the expedition, they're launching the skiffs,
and it seems they've got a couple wounded, though I can't
make out who, sir. They're down to the brown shallows of
the river, and there's some getting into the boats by the
jungle's edge.

RALEIGH

Get ready to brace them aboard. I'm coming down.

SAILOR

It's Captain Keymis's boat, sir, and there's two dead.

RALEIGH

Who are they?

SAILOR

I can't rightly tell, sir. They're dead is all I know.

RALEIGH

Give them a shout again!

(BERRIO *enters below.*)

SAILOR

Allo there! Alloa off there!

(*Silence.*)

CHORUS

Now the hot wind haunts the abandoned armour,
The wild bees build in the rusting Spanish helms,
The armoured cricket nests in the empty shield.

SAILOR

Allo, allo there? Who got it this time, mate?

VOICE OFF

Jeremy Ford, carpenter. Walter Raleigh, squire.

BERRIO (*Moving forward.*)

Señor!

RALEIGH

What is it now, man? Do you come to mock me?

SAILOR

It's the boy, sir. They're coming aboard.

(*The* PATROL *boards,* KEYMIS *enters; behind,*
SAILORS *bearing* SON's *body.*)

SAILOR

Come, rest him on the table, I'll shift the lute.

KEYMIS

Your son is dead, my lord.

RALEIGH

And gold outlasts the wearer. Remain here, Keymis.
          (*All exit but* BERRIO *and* KEYMIS.)
Will you not go into your quarters?

BERRIO

Suffering binds men together, Excellency.
Not long ago I mourned my nephew's death.

RALEIGH

How did this happen?

KEYMIS

He fell in the skirmish with another sailor
When we attacked the fort of San Thome.

RALEIGH

I placed the boy in your particular care.
               (*Over body*)
So late I heard thee playing on the lute;
Now these poor fingers, that should pluck a viol,
Are cold as this sword that I place in them.
There he lies, on the unknown world, my son.

KEYMIS

We must return to England now, Sir Walter.

RALEIGH

I weigh this body of my finished son
Against, sweet Christ, a little mound of gold,
But God, who sacrificed Thy Son Thyself,
Temper my grief, rib me with fortitude.
O death that takes a little piece of me,
When one man dies, the only empire is yours.
All mockery carved in that marble stiffness
Wrapped in the reputation of a shroud,
A mirror clouded by the breath of time.
A broken sword laid at the foot of war,
A cold meat for the whimsy of a king
                    (*Pause.*)
—Keymis!

KEYMIS

I share your sorrow, Walter, I am with you.

RALEIGH (*Turning on him.*)

With me? I wish you were with him there dead.

KEYMIS

And I. Believe me, as his friend and captain.

RALEIGH

Or to speak the truth, his captain and his butcher.

KEYMIS

Butcher? I know the quantity of your suffering,
But I was his friend when he lived. You know it.

RALEIGH

Take him away, the lute, map, everything; but Keymis,
If you are as honest as you say you are, then look,
And take his murder as your own negligence.
                    (*The body is borne away.*)
Come back here, man!

KEYMIS

Do you call me back to abuse me, then, Sir Walter,
Here in the full view of the common sailors,
To the contempt and pity of the enemy?

RALEIGH

Yes, yes, and more, death is a common thing,
And it is you who are the enemy.

KEYMIS

                    Your mind is feverish.

RALEIGH

It was you, with your cupidinous, common fawning,
Who drew me by the sleeve away from God
When I was locked in darkness in the tower,
And whispered gold and empire in this ear.

KEYMIS

Whatever fever you may have, Sir Walter, I tell you,
That is a weak and cowardly lie, sweet Christ. Remember,
We searched for Guiana many times before this.
Then it was dear Laurence, friend, exchanger of my love.
It was your fever that infected mine. We have failed,
And execution waits for us in England. But God,
I had preferred to slaughter Indians uselessly
Than to endure this malice from a gentleman.

BERRIO

Gentlemen, señores. I lost a nephew to your soldiers.

RALEIGH

I'll tell you, de Berrio, the contagion of madness
Makes snakes of friends when profit is involved
(Points.)
There is the leech Keymis who fed on me,
Who crawled on green Guiana like a leaf,
Murdering men's sons and fattening on my friendship.
Do not cross my sight till we return to England.
(He exits.)

KEYMIS

O God, pluck down the star of selfish men!
Break the proud shaft on which they hoist their colours.
The man has burst my heart. I loved them both.
I could not hold the boy back, I swear to God.

I roll the map up, where the stain of his life
Marks red for conquest. I will not live with this.

(He exits.)

BERRIO

Again and again, the plot of conquest follows
The hollow carcass of the drum of reputation,
Who weeps for Jeremy Ford?

(Enter two SAILORS.*)*

FIRST SAILOR

If you please, sir. Come, mate, give us a hand.

BERRIO

What is the matter now?

SECOND SAILOR

If you please, sir. Captain Keymis has just killed hisself.

FIRST SAILOR

There's some takes things too hard. Excuse us, Governor.

(BERRIO *bends his head over the table. The* SAILORS *wait.
Slow fade-out. Drum.*)

Interlude

POMPEY (*Rushing out onstage.*)

Mano! Hey, Mano. Where this man gone now?
I bet you he with them big shot in the five-dollar seat.

MANO (*Emerging.*)

What happen now, pardner? You ain't tired harass me?

POMPEY

You know what I wanted to tell you, pardner?

MANO

I don't want to hear nothing.

POMPEY

Don't vex nuh, pal. Is this. That last sailor there who carry
off the table, the second one.

MANO

You mean the squinge-faced fellow?

POMPEY

Yeah, heself, well—

MANO

Well, what?

POMPEY

You ain't find he talk like a Bajan?

MANO

Oh God, is that you call a man out here for, and people looking?

POMPEY (*Sitting on barrel.*)

Looking at this feller, you know, remind me of a old joke once about a Barbadian.

MANO

Look nuh, man, we ain't have time for that now.

POMPEY

This joke happen way back in about 1618 or so, the year Raleigh dead. Or some time around there. (MANO *moves away.*) Wait nuh, man, I sure you going enjoy this joke. It have history in it. (MANO *comes back.*) They had this Bajan feller during the early days of slavery, when some of the British islands was being settled, you know, like St. Kitts, Antigua, St. Lucia, and so on and so on.

MANO

I gone, yes.

POMPEY

Well, this feller, he get a work. This wasn't no ordinary kind a work, you know. He wasn't no *Nègre jardin*, no plantation nigger. He was a wine steward on a big estate.

MANO

You ever give a short joke yet?

POMPEY

Well, one night he bounce up wid a drunken sailor.

MANO (*Moving away.*)

Look, nuh, like you planning to sleep here tonight?

POMPEY

All right, all right. But stop! You think I was lying? Look the two of them there! You going see if I was lying.

(*They exit.*)

Scene 7

Night. A wharf—enter a SAILOR, *jug in hand—Barbados.*

SAILOR

It's midnight, and I can't find the way to the ship, and I wouldn't like to be stuck in the Barbados for nothing. It's pitch black and I've too much rum in me drum to move farther. Hup, boys, hup, boys! It's no use, me legs is buckling below me like a shivered keel. Perhaps, and I'm lucky, I'll get a passerby to pick me up. It's a pitch-dark alley. Ah!

(*A prim* NEGRO STEWARD *passes with a small crate, sees the* SAILOR, *sneers; then passes on.* SAILOR *rises.*)

SAILOR

Hey you, nigger! give us a hand there, mate.

Hey, you, come back here. You, buck, give us a hand.

STEWARD (*Long pause, sneers.*)

Talking to me?

SAILOR

Yes, mate. I'm on me way to the ship, aren't you a nigger?
I can't hardly make out complexions in this obscurity.

STEWARD

Give you a hand? You should be ashamed of yourself.
(*Moves off.*)

SAILOR

Hey, you can't go off, I compel you to give me a hand.

STEWARD (*Setting down the cask carefully.*)

Now look. You see here yourself, mister man! If you can't
ack like a gentleman in a respectable British colony, then all
I could say to you is you should be ashamed of yourself. A
sailor of His Majesty's navy, a Englishman, and drunk as a
lord on the demon rum. And look here, too, besides, friend.
I not one of these common nigger men you see working
down by the carenage hauling spiders and getting on like
they ain't got self-respeck for their owners, yuh! I works at
Sir George Somers's cousin's as house, food, and wine steward, so hence the uniform which I intends to respeck! A

Englishman like you cavorting in this public alley on a Sunday night!

(*The* SAILOR *recoils from the outburst.*)

SAILOR

Look, mate, it's late and I'm due aboard.

STEWARD

I don't care what time it is, this is the year 1618, and this is a British colony, and Barbados is not one of them loose-living other colonies in these islands with their riotous living, like Jamaica and the buccaneers, and the other places, this is a decent self-respecking colony with a sense of justice and decency. You not in St. Kitts, Antigua, or St. Lucia, or one of them nasty French places, and I consider you should be ashamed of yourself! You have a responsibility to protect these British colonies with vessels, and so discharge them according to your service, before I take your name and number! Imagine, shouting my name out in the middle of the night like some bewildered alley cat. I am a steward, in a decent conducted plantation, and house-proud. Why, you getting on like one of them convicts and indentured Englishmen that they send out to work in the colonies. Now get up and march. You villain. Get up, I say, and remember the flag you fly under, you wicked thing you, and give me that bottle. On, get on. You villainous thing you. The ship is yonder. Now garn, garn. (*Pushes* SAILOR *off.*) A sailor of His Majesty and drunk! (*He exits.*)

Scene 8
The Death of Raleigh

1618. Cold dawn. The Tower of London. Enter RALEIGH.
Behind him a PRIEST *and an* EXECUTIONER.
Drumbeat.

RALEIGH

The wind is sharp, keen as an axe's edge.

PRIEST

Sir Walter, now is the time
When you must fit your vessel for that fatal sea,
To that Virginian voyage, death's New Found Land.
Yet Christ shall guard you.

RALEIGH

Do you hear that, executioner?
Make no arrangements for my supper tonight.
Come, lead me to the summit of all endeavour.

PRIEST

God keep you on that long voyage, Sir Walter.

RALEIGH

I had forgotten God too long, my age is finished,
Just as de Berrio said, as the old sailor warned
At my son's cost, and broken Laurence Keymis.
I'll tell you this, Father, although my hermit's voice

Will be drowned in the roar of wars and politics,
The only wisdom, whether of single man or nation,
Is to study the brevity of this life and love it.
That's the poor wisdom I bequeath to soldiers.
If I sound unreasonable, sir, it is because, again,
I have lost my head. Look, I get not even a dry laugh.

EXECUTIONER

Come.

(*They climb the steps.* RALEIGH *places his head on the block.
Drums to crescendo. Blackout.*)

(*Enter* CHORUS *in single spot.*)

CHORUS

The blood that jets from Raleigh's severed head
Lopped like a rose when England's strength was green,
Spreads on the map its bright imperial red
To close the stain of conquest on our scene.
So Time turns now from Europe and the sea,
Revolves its gaze and shows the land itself,
Hundreds of battles past the discovery,
To the slaves' suffering and the settlers' wealth,
Until an exiled people find release,
Through revolutions of despair and love,
As human suffering presages peace.
How shall we love, till we have known love's cost,

How praise our liberty, so lately earned,
How shall our brothers love, till we forgive?
And so to Haiti now our theme is turned.
How shall we live, till these ghosts bid us live?

(*Fade-out. Music.*)

Scene 9

Haiti. GENERAL LECLERC*'s mansion.* M. ARMAND
CALIXTE-BREDA; *his nephew,* ANTON, *apart.* GENERAL
LECLERC, GENERAL *and* MADAME DE ROUVRAY.
Liveried NEGRO LACKEYS. *Night. The garden.*
Wine is served.

LECLERC

It's not quite as terrible as one had imagined,
This heat, I mean, General. In France one had heard
That Haiti was a plague of fevers and sweltering heat,
Yet your garden is cool, and the view is excellent.

DE ROUVRAY

You will find it almost wintry later, in the mountains.
You can imagine what terrain it is for a revolt.
I have very little sentiment in surrendering my command.

LECLERC

And you, Madame de Rouvray?

MADAME DE ROUVRAY
                    You know wives, General Leclerc.
This is what I shall miss, the supervision of my gardens,
I hope Madame Pauline will look after these lilies.
Monsieur Calixte, I know, will understand my misery,
Being himself the paragon of planters.

CALIXTE-BREDA
                    I can understand, madame.
I comprehend completely your devotion to lilies.

MADAME DE ROUVRAY
And since Madame Pauline is absent, General,
Perhaps you can tell us of the situation in Paris.

DE ROUVRAY
She probably means the fashions, but, my dear Emilie,
General Leclerc is more proficient at uprooting rebellions
Than in describing Paris couture and the qualities of flowers.

LECLERC
It has altered considerably since the birth of the republic.
But Calixte's nephew has returned, full of enthusiasm,
So perhaps Monsieur Anton—it is Anton, is it not, monsieur?
Perhaps this silent gentleman is the best one to ask.

MADAME DE ROUVRAY
Haiti has also altered. Things are terribly unsettled.
Is there much similarity, in your opinion, Anton?

(ANTON *moves away.*)

CALIXTE-BREDA

When Anton drinks too much wine, as he did here at dinner,
The boy falls into an unshakeable melancholy.

MADAME DE ROUVRAY

Do you think Madame Leclerc may have met with an
    accident?
It is dangerous to be riding these roads at night alone.

LECLERC (*Smiles.*)

My wife is not alone. I think she should be safe.

DE ROUVRAY

You see there is always the danger of runaway slaves;
Then, there are serpents . . .

MADAME DE ROUVRAY

                And so many other dangers, monsieur.
There are hazards much more subtle in a colonial society.

CALIXTE-BREDA (*Laughs.*)

I resent that word, excuse me, "colonial."

MADAME DE ROUVRAY (*Fanning.*)

                Oh, quite innumerable hazards.
The danger, though concealed of a mixed aristocracy,
The ambushes that wait for one under glittering candles,

The serpents in the smiles of the most charming hostess,
Arrows of eyebrows, and artilleries of slander
Behind the barricades of those fluttering fans . . .

LECLERC

        You don't like the word "colonial"?
This, I presume, then, is the birth of a nation?
Generals who were slaves, each one a black Spartacus.
You know, Napoleon calls them gilded Africans.

DE ROUVRAY

They are becoming quite formal in their conduct of this
    war.

LECLERC (*Impatiently*)

This is not a war, de Rouvray, it is a large-scale civic
    action.
I am employed to subjugate a province of France.

ANTON

                Do not be so sure,
One must never underrate the authority of the people.

CALIXTE-BREDA

Slaves are not people, they are intelligent animals.

MADAME DE ROUVRAY

Gentlemen, please, let us not lose our tempers.

ANTON

Madame, I am simply saying this is not a revolt.

LECLERC

So at last we grow eloquent. You say the will of the people.
Let us tell you, monsieur, that that expression is a fallacy.
Remember it was the people who demanded Barabbas.

ANTON

This is the philosophic corruption of power.

CALIXTE-BREDA

Anton, you are a guest.

LECLERC

It is a fact, nevertheless, despite your enthusiasm,
The people have always chosen their particular demon.
They created their Caesar as they created Napoleon.
But you have been reading Rousseau and Montesquieu,
They are romantics overcome by the odours of the mob.

ANTON (*Impatiently*)

This is Caesarism.

DE ROUVRAY

Anton, it's discussion.

ANTON

That is monarchy. And you, a republican.

LECLERC

You sound angry, young man. I am a cynic who worships
    order.
I doubt such things exist as liberty or good marriages.
Don't you consider yourself superior to your uncle's
    Negroes?

ANTON (*Controlling himself.*)

Monsieur, you are a general, and your industry is death,
But there is a new spirit that walks over the earth.

LECLERC

I know, I was part of it. *Liberté, égalité, fraternité.*
And what has this turned into but democratic despotism?

CALIXTE-BREDA (*Smiling.*)

Then you believe in the monarchy? Or are you testing our
    allegiance?

LECLERC

Show me a good man and I will show you a good nation.
Do you know what will happen if your revolution succeeds?
There will not be liberty but mere patterns of revenge.
The history of man is founded on human nature, and
We cannot exorcise the guilt of original sin.

DE ROUVRAY

Does the First Consul know what opinions you hold, General?

LECLERC

What does it matter? I am an excellent general,
And then I am fortunate, my wife is Caesar's sister.
And here in good time, she arrives with a new province.

(*Enter* PAULINE LECLERC *with young officer.*)

PAULINE

Now I shall not say anything dull or unpredictable
But that I forgot all about it, or say I remembered
How monotonous the conversation of generals can be;
I have a haphazard memory, and so all is forgiven.
This is Lieutenant Foujade; my husband, General Leclerc;
Your commander, General de Rouvray; Madame de Rouvray.
This is Monsieur Calixte. Oh, this is so absurd,
          (*Before* ANTON)
And this . . .

CALIXTE-BREDA

My nephew, madame. Monsieur Anton Calixte.

PAULINE

Oh yes, yes indeed. Can I have a drink with you?
Lieutenant Foujade is an authority on Haiti.
We toured a few estates, including yours, Monsieur Calixte.
He knows all about factories, we toured the compounds,
So if I reek a little of the *parfum d'Afrique*,
Endure it gently. There seems to have been trouble.

CALIXTE-BREDA

It is normal, they shake the chains a little.

LIEUTENANT FOUJADE

It seemed worse than that, monsieur.

              A few seem to have escaped.

CALIXTE-BREDA

           There are ways of retrieving them,
It is an industrial hazard. There are dogs, you observe.

PAULINE

How was dinner, Madame de Rouvray? I am so sorry,
    forgive me?

MADAME DE ROUVRAY

Not at all.

LIEUTENANT FOUJADE

If you will excuse me, messieurs, madame.
Please accept my apologies, sir, but we were delayed.

LECLERC

C'est normal.

       (*Exit* LIEUTENANT FOUJADE.)
Now, if Monsieur Calixte will accompany us.
We can talk out these problems with a tour of the garden
And leave your eloquent nephew to chat with the ladies.
Nothing is more monotonous than the small talk of soldiers.

You say, then, de Rouvray, that the most efficient generals,
For want of a better term, are this fellow Boukmann,
Dessalines, and . . . the other . . . what's his name?

DE ROUVRAY

Christophe . . . Monsieur Calixte knows all about this also.
He has helped me enormously, he knows the country
   thoroughly . . .
I hate mountain country, you never finish a war . . .

(*Exit* GENERALS *and* CALIXTE-BREDA.)

PAULINE

Then are you packed and ready for Paris, madame?

MADAME DE ROUVRAY

Yes, but I feel so archaic, so dated in the fashion.
I trust Haiti will not bore you, it is different from Paris.
There is little to do that one can call civilised.
It is rich, but vulgar, as you may well have observed.

PAULINE

Oh, one creates one's pleasures to suit every country.
But what does one do that is different from Paris?
I have grown so tired of false dukes and society.

MADAME DE ROUVRAY

What does one do in fact that is not imitation?
Perhaps Anton could tell us. Men have all the liberties.

ANTON

Is madame in search of something exciting and different?

PAULINE

It begins to sound exciting before you even describe it.

ANTON

Then I must have another glass before I proceed.
But as a general's wife, I am sure you have seen much.
Industrial hazard, as my uncle observed . . .

MADAME DE ROUVRAY

                              Anton is still sullen,
He has just lost an argument to your husband.

PAULINE

Do not mind my husband, he is cynical and dispassionate.
But tell us, monsieur.

ANTON

                    Well, quite recently, madame,
We have devised a spectacle of epic proportions.
            (*Pauses, studies their faces.*)
There is a place in the city, designed like an arena,
Half shadow in the afternoon, say, on some boring Sunday—
Sunday afternoons are the same in every part of the
      world—
Where a carnivorous spectacle is gaining popularity.

MADAME DE ROUVRAY (*Agitatedly*)

Anton, please. Madame Leclerc did not mean that.

ANTON

The Negroes, you know, are punished in public.
They are led into his arena, as in a public circus,
And then, with some brief ceremony, the theatre
    commences . . .

MADAME DE ROUVRAY

If you will excuse me, I must finish my packing.
It is getting late, and there are things I must do.
Good night, madame; good night, Anton.
              (*She exits.*)

PAULINE

              You were saying, monsieur?

ANTON

The most popular scene in this comic spectacle:
Gunpowder is poured into noses, ears, and mouths.
Then the actors are fixed into farcical positions,
Then the powder is lit, and the victims are exploded.
              (*Laughs.*)
Of course, no one is permitted to act his role twice.
Is that sufficient?

PAULINE

        If you have finished.

ANTON

Do not miss the meaning, there are other diversions,
For there is this ballet of putting them into holes.

PAULINE

Holes?

ANTON

Des grands trous, comme ça.
They are buried in the ground to their necks in these holes.
They are then smeared with honey and the ants erode them.
There is some species of ant that can strip human flesh;
Then often there are dogs, which are trained for that purpose.
That is our theatre, but it is rather repetitious.

PAULINE

It is not worse than war. Have you watched it yourself?

ANTON (*Sits.*)

That is why I can describe it, I am torn apart also.
My head is reeling, and I feel very drunk. It is horrible.

PAULINE

Then why do you watch it?

ANTON

Why, madame? I will tell you why.
Because I am torn to pieces with them, I am myself a division.
By the fact that I am half African and half French,

I must become both spectator and victim. It is amusing.
Don't you understand what I am telling you, madame?
I am not the nephew of Monsieur Armand Calixte; I am
His son, illegitimate; all society knows this, but
It is not said directly.

PAULINE

Who is your mother, then?

ANTON

She was a slave of his mansion.
He recognised her in darkness, in that republic
And that act in which complexions do not matter.
What do I do? Many years ago, I was tempted to admit it,
To be what I am and not be ashamed, a Haitian.
Then I saw our two delegates to the French General Assembly,
Ogé and Chavannes, broken on the wheel in public.
I do not know why I am telling you all this.

PAULINE

You are upset, monsieur; come and sit down a little.
And you do not understand why you are telling me this?

ANTON

Should I speak the truth to you, Madame Leclerc?

PAULINE

Yes, it is still the best thing, to follow one's impulses,
To avoid hurting others and destroying one's sanity.

ANTON

Look, we own an excellent coachman, his name is Toussaint,
He is a Negro of a most remarkable docility.
I know he loves my father, he loves me as his son,
But since such cruelty and this new liberty of man
Have made Haiti a crisis in the history of this age,
I have seen his black face tormented with division,
Between duty to his people and the love of our family.
How am I better than Toussaint, greater than his anguish?
Compared to him I am nothing. Do you know what I
    should do?
I should hate all this elegance, to sit among the slaves,
Be mocked for an ape, be torn apart by dogs,
Than to be choked to death with these silks . . .

(*He struggles with his collar.*)

PAULINE

                    Anton, please, please . . .
    (*Pause.*)
Is that all you wish to tell me?

ANTON

You know it is not all. How can that be all?
    (*Pause.*)
Since the first night I saw you, the centre of attention
In the glittering ballroom at Madame de Rouvray's
    mansion,
Barricaded by lieutenants, and then once again tonight,

White and lovely as the moon, and equally remote,
My body trembled at the minute of your entrance.

(GENERAL LECLERC *appears on the balcony above.*)

PAULINE

You talk too much, Anton.

ANTON

I must talk of these things.

PAULINE

No, let them go; as women do, take life as it comes.

ANTON

And yes, and this destroys me, I try to understand things,
But it is sad, it is sad, the whole thing is sad.
It is sad to see belief contradicted by necessity,
It is sad to see new countries making old mistakes.
One could hope from the past the present would be simple,
But it is sad to see only the repetition of desire.

PAULINE (*Taking his head to her bosom.*)
It is like the first years of love, understanding is hard . . .
There now, let me kiss you; forget the hate of this world.
Learn to love one person and your view will be mellowed.

(*They kiss.* LECLERC *descends, unseen.*)

TOUSSAINT (*Enters.*)

Monsieur Anton. *Ton père te demande.*

ANTON

This is our coachman, Toussaint. What is it?

LECLERC (*Emerging.*)

It appears there is some trouble again on his estate,
The slaves are burning the canes, you can see the glow.
There behind the mountains. He is rather anxious, he wants
You to help him with a hunt. I'll lend him soldiers.

ANTON

I cannot help him, sir. *Dîtes lui ma kai venir Toussaint.*
I am not going. I shall walk back to the estate. *Allez.*

TOUSSAINT

Monsieur Anton . . .

ANTON

Allez, allez. I am not hunting tonight.
(*Exit* TOUSSAINT.)
It is not far, I know a path through the fields.

LECLERC

Do you think that you are in any condition to walk?
I can lend you a horse if you insist on returning.

ANTON

No, I am going alone. I thank you. Good night, good night,
madame.

(*He exits.*)

LECLERC

A remarkable young man, very stubborn, very passionate.

PAULINE

I presume that you saw us kissing from the balcony.

LECLERC

We retain our understanding, I am your brother's general,
And you remain his ambassador for foreign affairs.

(*They go off. Glare of fire—drums. Lights fade out.*)

Scene 10

Night. ANTON, *drunk in the canefields, walking alone.
A glare in the sky.*

ANTON (*Singing.*)
*Oh, the moon may be a silver coin,
And the sun is a sovereign light.*
(*He stops, laughs.*)
The moon, the moon, it was that remarkable metaphor
of the moon that startled her. Anton, you are a fool. She

slaughters men as her husband does battalions . . . Well, she has uprooted me also. You are drunk and a fool. Oh, let me thank my fool of a father, Monsieur Armand Calixte, otherwise how should I have met her? Ah well, I have done this before, only I will not hunt men like animals, I am not a hunter of men. What was that sound? It seems as if the whole country is on fire. I think I must be lost. Think, if I were not of this complexion now, she and that fat Madame de Rouvray and her stupid husband would have been amused to see me exploded with saltpetre, ripped by hounds. Ha. Life is ironic . . .

(*During this speech, three black figures creep near* ANTON.)

VOICES (*Softly, like the wind*)
Anton Calixte! Anton Calixte! Anton Calixte!

ANTON (*Alert*)
                                                    Who was that?
Yes, yes, I am Anton Calixte, what do you want?

VOICE
You are the son of Monsieur Calixte?

ANTON
I am his nephew. His nephew! I know these voices!
I am one of you, believe me. My mother was black, my
    mother was black.
Gaspar, Félicien? . . .

VOICES (*Like wind as they circle him.*)
You have the blood of your father, for that you will die.
When the moon hides in a cloud, for that you will die.

ANTON (*Urgent*)
Let me see who you are. I have done nothing to you.
Oh God! I have your blood in me.

(*The moon hides in a cloud. They murder him. A* SLAVE
screams in triumph. The drums of revolution begin.)

Scene 11

The Bois Cayman. Drums. Enter SLAVES *running with
flambeaux towards the body. Silence. Enter* BOUKMANN.

BOUKMANN

Jour sang rivé!

SLAVES

Hallelujah!

BOUKMANN

Jour nègre rivé!

SLAVES

Hallelujah!

BOUKMANN

C'est moi Boukmann qui dit ça!
Dire Hosannah!

SLAVES

Hosannah!

BOUKMANN (*Holding up cross.*)

Ça c'est croix n'hommes blancs, pas croix Damballa!

SLAVES

Hallelujah!
C'est pas croix Damballa!

BOUKMANN

Crasez croix Dieu blanc.
(*He breaks the cross.*)
You wishes to know why Boukmann break the cross?
This is the white God cross, not the god of this colour.
Alors, crasez croix Dieu blanc
Hosez serpent Damballa.

(*Drums. A serpent is brought in.*)

SLAVES

Damballa, Damballa!

(*A white rooster is brought in by a* FEMALE SLAVE.)

BOUKMANN (*Holding the rooster.*)

Red blood will flow from the white throat, I say.

Burn the canes, kill the enemies,

Kill everything white in Haiti today!

(*A ritual dance begins, with flambeaux.*)

We forget our gods when we leave Africa.

We make Shango vex, we forget *Damballa!*

Brûlez, brûlez, brûlez!

(*All exit, led by* BOUKMANN, *with torches. Drumming.
The dead body is left abandoned.* TOUSSAINT, *as a
coachman, enters, finds* ANTON *dead.*)

TOUSSAINT

Monsieur Anton! Anton, Monsieur Anton?

(*Over the body*)

Monsieur Anton! Drunk again. Come on, *levez.*

(*He touches blood.*)

Oh God. My other life is finished. Love is dead.

(*He takes up the body.*)

This poor boy hated nothing, nothing.

(*A* SLAVE WOMAN *enters, passes* TOUSSAINT.)

SLAVE WOMAN

That's a heavy burden you're carrying, black man.

(*Fade-out.*)

Scene 12

*It is the late autumn of the first year of the nineteenth
century. Rebel Haitian armies under Toussaint sack the
city of Les Cayes. Bands of marauders. Torrential rain
fights with the fire of the city.* DESSALINES, *soaked,
watches the scene with some* OFFICERS. *A shed.*
A SOLDIER *passes.*

DESSALINES

You there, *soldat*!

SOLDIER

Yes, my general.

DESSALINES

Under what army are you, me, Christophe, which, *hein*?

SOLDIER

With General Toussaint, General Dessalines.

DESSALINES

In your cloak there, rum, *non*? Bring it here, *nègre*, and
give your general a drink. Look at it burn, look. Remember
this, this is the turning of a century, *nègre*. Oh, it pleases
me. I could wash my face, Sergeant, in the handful of its
ashes. Tell me, I love to hear it, what city is that? (*He
drinks.*)

SOLDIER

That is Les Cayes, *mon général*, and we have scattered the
forces of the mulatto Rigaud. The worst enemy of our new
black republic.

DESSALINES

There must be one hundred thousand slaughtered there.
Burn, burn, city of contagions, consume it all.
Though God poured out the whole basin of this sky
He could not drench that fire. Go, leave the bottle.
You, there, you soldiers. In what quarter of the town
Is General Christophe?

SOLDIER

Here he comes now, my general.

(*Enter* CHRISTOPHE *muddy, tired.*)

DESSALINES

Put up the general's tent to break this rain.
(*An awning is added to the balcony.*)
Look at it, General. It is art, is it not?

CHRISTOPHE (*Collapses on a stool.*)
Poor country. This is not a war.

DESSALINES

No, it is not war. But it will do for now. Here, drink!
I understand you had a difficult assault?

CHRISTOPHE

> You said assault?

This butchering of mulattos you call assault?
You'll catch a chill there, sitting in the rain.
Lend me a cloth, my own is soaked with blood.

DESSALINES

Here, have this shirt, I sent for dry boots and linen.
Well, where is our excellent commander L'Ouverture?

CHRISTOPHE

I thought that he was working close to you.

DESSALINES

> No, I had an easy quarter.

A cowardly segment of Rigaud's mulatto army. Oh, look!
There must be one hundred thousand dead out there.
Listen to the cries.

CHRISTOPHE

> Yes, they smell wonderful, don't they?

Burnt flesh and trampled muck and sweating rain.
It is only two o'clock, and dark as an eclipse.

DESSALINES

The pot is overturned, up in the north; the news is this,
That bloody, murderous slaughterer Sonthonax,
Boukmann, the Jamaican, and other rebellious regiments
Have burned the plains into a smoking shambles.

CHRISTOPHE

They burn the crops, but when peace has returned . . .
And which of them has yet conquered Leclerc?

DESSALINES

Up in the north two thousand whites are slaughtered.
The flame is catching in the unharvested canes,
Not only in this island, but through the Antilles.
We have sent agents to stir up this violence. Drink, drink.
Here, two hundred estates destroyed. The black wolves
Of our marauding soldiers, swollen by famine,
Have sacked the indigo and coffee fields. It will spread
Even in the British territories. In Martinique, Guadeloupe.

CHRISTOPHE

I only wish I had your sense of theatre. And Leclerc,
What has he offered us for the capture of Toussaint?

DESSALINES

The yellow fever has wrecked the French battalions.
The time has come, with Leclerc's forces weakened,
For us to strike some temporary pact. As you remember,
He offered to withdraw his forces of occupation
If we hand over Toussaint to Napoleon. Oh, this Napoleon,
He is such an egotist. He thinks that Toussaint's capture
Would weaken us. Oh, *mon Dieu, mi blague*, I could laugh,
    laugh.

CHRISTOPHE

There is no one the Corsican hates more than this ape,
This—what does he call him?—"this gilded African." We
sell him?

DESSALINES

One thing perturbs me. Pass me the bottle, friend.
One thing perturbs poor Dessalines: we are four armies,
And all assembled under distinctive generals, you, me,
Toussaint, Maurepas. But of all of us, Toussaint
Has grown most power drunk. He has monarchic aims, I
know.

CHRISTOPHE

Let us not lie to ourselves. We are betraying him.
A transaction of exchange, let us not excuse it, *hein*?
You think he'll set himself up as Emperor?
How do you know?

DESSALINES (*Laughs.*)

I have a parrot that speaks to me in my dreams. Look!
Napoleon thinks of the whole world as his empire, yet
This ape has beaten him, outwitted his best generals.
And since Napoleon thinks in terms of a late Caesar,
He thinks this ape, encaged, will resolve the war.
Even Leclerc, who is a cynic and no fool, believes it.
And as you say, this is not war. Yet how I love it,
Look at it burn. This is more than war, it is revolt;
It is a new age, the black man's turn to kill.

CHRISTOPHE

        Then we are no better. Revenge
Is very tiring. Please do not hog the bottle.
Where does all that leave the mulatto, Dessalines?

DESSALINES (*Pointing.*)

There, out there dead in the stinking rain.
    (*A drumbeat. Enter* TOUSSAINT.)
Speak, parrot. Here comes our bill of sale. The meat we
    dice for.

TOUSSAINT (*To the* OFFICERS)

We have scattered Rigaud, but we still have enemies
Here on the soil of our beloved Haiti: Leclerc, his armies;
Yet we have allies also, the fever, and our great zeal
To make this country greater than it was. Revenge is
    nothing.
Peace, the restoration of the burnt estates, the ultimate
Rebuilding of those towns war has destroyed, peace is harder.
We strike our march in the next hour. Collect your troops.

(*A bugle is blown.* OFFICERS *exit.*)

DESSALINES

Your lungs are iron, to still have breath to speak. Some rum?

TOUSSAINT

These clothes are stuck to me with filth and blood, a basin.
No, I must keep a clear head, though my generals do not.

DESSALINES

How many did you butcher of the yellow ones?

(*A* SOLDIER *brings a basin and a cloth.*)

TOUSSAINT

        I do not have my ledgers with me.
The cavalry is cutting the last troops on the plain;
There is nothing between our mercy and their death
But a vast swamp of stinking mud. It is dark,
Dark as a portent at this turn of the year, the birth
Of a new century. What comes at the end of it, my friends?

CHRISTOPHE

This is a new age, born like us, in blood . . .

TOUSSAINT

        Yes, yes, but I hate excess.
(*He washes his hands.*)

DESSALINES (*Roars with laughter.*)

Ho, ha! He kills ten thousand or more defenceless citizens
Who did him no harm but that their colour was wrong
And shrugs his shoulders and says he hates excess. Oh, oh
I love, I kiss this hypocrite!

TOUSSAINT (*Angrily*)

        I am not a hypocrite, Jean Jacques,
I hate this now it is all finished. I remember

The body of the first mulatto I ever saw. The son
Of a stupid planter called Calixte. Multiply that.
I come from an exhausting expedition and I find
My two best generals getting drunk like sergeants.
Go, collect your forces, I want to think a little.

(*Exit* CHRISTOPHE, DESSALINES.)

Oh God, that I should find the centre of this whirlwind,
Those leaves of yellow bodies whirled in wind.

(*Enter* TWO SOLDIERS, CALIXTE-BREDA
in rags between them.)

SOLDIER

We found this one hiding in the ruins, General.
What shall we do with him?

TOUSSAINT

    I do not know the man . . . who . . .
Calixte? Is it Monsieur Calixte?

CALIXTE-BREDA (*Shaking free from the* SOLDIERS.)
    And it is General Toussaint, is it not?
The conqueror of Haiti . . . I want to talk with you,
Unless the general must go back to his butchering.

TOUSSAINT

You soldiers, stand in easy distance from this tent.
What are you doing in Les Cayes? You live in the north?

(*The* SOLDIERS *withdraw.*)

CALIXTE-BREDA

There is no north. They have burnt the good land.
You should know that, it is you who guide this war.

TOUSSAINT (*Holding out the bottle.*)

Here, have a drink of rum. I do not know what savour,
You may remember how one improved its vintage
With an occasional slave tossed in the vats?

CALIXTE-BREDA (*Hanging his head.*)

I was never cruel. It was the times, the thought.

TOUSSAINT

I am not cruel either. It is also in my case the times,
The compulsion of opinion. I did not begin it.

CALIXTE-BREDA (*Angrily*)

You call this compulsion, this slaughtering of children,
This dedicated erasure of any complexion?
I have walked through the smoking fields, through the
    burnt land
That we all loved, destroyed, that was once green,
Racked by a rabble, turned savage as wild pigs.

TOUSSAINT (*Shouting.*)

They are my soldiers, not pigs, not animals.

CALIXTE-BREDA

I stepped across hacked citizens in these streets,
Blind in a stream of tears, I moved through fire,
Oh God in heaven, Toussaint, hell is not worse.

TOUSSAINT

War is not a drawing-room minuet.

CALIXTE-BREDA

Do not call this war, you hypocritical liar!
Since the day Anton died, and you abandoned him
On the white columned steps of Mal Maison,
I have pursued your great career with diligence.
I heard of how you joined the marauding armies,
Who burnt our lands and shambled the green north;
Your rise in the field of battle; how you wrecked Maitland
And drove the English down to the sea. Until today,
You are blood drunk, since that first boy you murdered.

TOUSSAINT

Murdered? Boy?

CALIXTE-BREDA

My son, my son Anton, that was so far
You have forgotten it. You have seen so many dead,
Now that war makes your butchery legitimate.
(*He draws his pistol.*)

TOUSSAINT

Put down the pistol, Monsieur Calixte. Your son? What son?
He was your nephew then. Look, man, have you forgotten,
Is it because you're ruined you have turned pious?

CALIXTE-BREDA

O God, give me the strength to shoot this monster.

TOUSSAINT

And do not speak to me of God, monsieur; right now
I cannot think of God. Where was God in those years
When we were whipped and forced to eat our excrement,
Were peeled alive, pestered with carnivorous ants.
Where was God? All of a sudden from your nephew's body
You have grown a delicate orchid called a conscience.
And blame the times. I have learnt to pick up a child
Limp on my sword's edge as you would lift an insect;
I have to learn this. I love this land as well as you,
But when we tried this, when we tried to love you,
Where, O chaos, where was your heart?

CALIXTE-BREDA *(Weeping.)*

Toussaint, what, what is all this?
What is happening to the world, to Haiti?

(*A bugle sounds in the distance.*)

TOUSSAINT

Oh God, I do not know, Monsieur Calixte. I do not know.
I am pushed forward, lifted on the crest of the wave,

Then I am abandoned among the wreckage, while
The mass of guilty men say, Oh, Toussaint, he is gentle, good.
Leave him to clean it. Listen, the bugle blows the march.
We are striking out . . .

(*Enter* DESSALINES, CHRISTOPHE.)

DESSALINES

Who is this filthy white? A spy?
(*He seizes his pistol.*)

TOUSSAINT

I was his coachman once. Give me the pistol, General
Dessalines.

CHRISTOPHE

His coachman? Is he offering your old employment back?
I will search him for letters. Jacques, keep the pistol.

TOUSSAINT

You see how my generals trust me, monsieur.

(*The bugle again.*)

DESSALINES

There are no gentlemen in Haiti now.

CHRISTOPHE

He has no letters. Come, it is time to march.

CALIXTE-BREDA

You have become three mad dogs all of you.
So these are the great generals. Is this Dessalines?

DESSALINES (*Gripping* CALIXTE-BREDA.)

Yes, white man, this is Dessalines, the general
Who ripped the white heart from the flag of France.
Tell them you saw him when you get down to hell.
Come, General, we are giving this one too much privilege.

TOUSSAINT

I still command here, Dessalines. Release him!

SERGEANT (*Enters.*)

The armies are assembled and ready to march.

CHRISTOPHE

Sergeant, wait!

DESSALINES

Well, is this a parliament now?

CALIXTE-BREDA

Look, you, both of you; I will not be pushed, I will not!

DESSALINES

He hates excess. I remember.

CALIXTE-BREDA

Did you kill my son? Answer me that.

(*Pause.*)

TOUSSAINT

Take him away, Sergeant.

SERGEANT

And . . .

DESSALINES

And shoot him, hang him, anything, you fool!
We have an army waiting for this ruin.

SERGEANT

My general?

TOUSSAINT

Shoot him. Monsieur Calixte, it is the times.

CALIXTE-BREDA

General, blame man and not the times, not God . . .

(*Exit* SERGEANT *with* CALIXTE-BREDA.)

DESSALINES

Eh, all this argument for a white . . .

CHRISTOPHE

Jacques, in the name of God! Enough!

(TOUSSAINT *is weeping, shoulders shaking. A long*
pause.)

Peace will be full of sour memories.

(*The sound of gunfire.*)

DESSALINES

Eh, qui ça, memories. Life is very long.

(*Pause.* TOUSSAINT *exits.*)

You see? He is crumbling. We sell him to Leclerc.

Why do you study me so carefully, my good friend?

I see that parrot on your shoulder, like a crow.

CHRISTOPHE

You are growing sick in your own mind, Jean Jacques.

Once we have sold him to Leclerc, peace is assured.

And we will share our power to restore the peace.

Now, come, it looks suspicious to be here alone.

(*He exits.*)

DESSALINES

The tent is struck now. Yet if all were known,

The parrot Jacko screams in Jacques's black ear,

Trust men as far as I can throw this stone.

(*He exits, trailing the bottle. Bugle, marching,*
shouts, drums. Blackout.)

Scene 13

Jamaica, 1830. Martial drums change to merry Jamaican mento. A white PLANTER *chucks his "housekeeper,"* YETTE, *out of his great house, throwing her possessions after her.*

PLANTER (*Hurling baggage.*)

I don't want to see any more of you on this estate, unless you learn to keep your thieving hands off my gold and silver!

YETTE (*Picking up baggage.*)

All Jamaica know 'bout you, you good-for-nothing rascal! You and your self-righteousness. I going tell them about you, mister! They should call you Calico, you off-colour planter, you!

PLANTER

Now go on down the road and into Kingston, where you belong. Before I set the dogs on you. And here your things! I should never have encouraged you; away, go on.

YETTE

One day the sugar market going collapse, and don't come weeping on my shoulder then. I'm not any ordinary slave, yuh. I got good blood. You can't ruin Yette. Don't mind I have coloured blood in me, at least I respectable. My father never come here as no convict.

PLANTER

You better get out.

(*He exits.* YETTE *gathers up her bundles, grumbling.*)

WOMAN (*Passing. The first of several who have entered for
the next scene.*)
Wey wrong, mi love?

YETTE

You jes' clear out of me way, hear?
(*She exits.*)

Scene 14

*Jamaica, 1833. Secret meeting of a Christian mission. Two
slaves,* ELIJAH *and* AARON, *hold up a banner marked:*
TO DWELL TOGETHER IN UNITY: SOCIETY FOR THE
PROPAGATION OF THE GOSPEL IN JAMAICA AND THE
INDIES. SLAVES *gathering.* DEACON SALE *enters.*

ELIJAH

The coast is clear, brothers and sisters.
Come, Brother Aaron, give me a hand with this banner.
The meeting go start just now.

AARON (*Helping with the banner.*)
You ain't hear 'bout Brother Pompey, Brother Elijah?
De soldiers chasing him for scattering pamphlets
'Bout emancipation and riots, but don't let Deacon know.

ELIJAH

You mean Pompey the shoemaker? Ain't he was a pacific man?

AARON

Well, him rougher than Atlantic now. Pass out the hymn
books?

ELIJAH

What's the damn use passing hymn books
And oonoo cyant read?

AARON

Why you don' hush you' mouth?

ALL

Good evening, Deacon.

DEACON SALE

Any sight or sound of Brother Pompey, Brother Aaron?
He has never been absent from a secret meeting before.

AARON (*Exultantly*)

Him spreading righteousness right and left, Deacon.
Like white doves on this countryside, him scattering pamphlets.

ELIJAH

We best hurry the meeting, Deacon. Aaron, hush!
You know is against the law. I going watch for soldiers.

DEACON SALE

Thank you, Brother Elijah.

(*He climbs up the steps.*)

Brothers and sisters assembled in Christ, I will read you the text of this banner. Repeat it after me, and try and remember it, as if it were embroidered forever on your hearts. To dwell . . .

SLAVES (*Together*)

To dwell . . .

ELIJAH

You talking too loud, Deacon, this place crawling with militia.

DEACON SALE

Thanks, vigilant Brother Elijah. Together . . .

SLAVES (*Together*)

Together . . .

DEACON SALE

. . . in unity . . .

SLAVES (*Together*)

To dwell together in unity . . .

DEACON SALE

Moses is anointing the head of his brother Aaron in this text. How sweet and how pleasant it is for brethren to dwell together in unity, it is like the precious ointment upon the head that ran down upon the beard, even Aaron's beard, that went down to the skirts of his garments. Oh, my poor, naked, abused brothers in Christ, today there are many in England who pray and work for your emancipation. What was that moaning in the night, Brother Elijah?

ELIJAH

Nothing, Deacon. The canes in the wind.

DEACON SALE

As a woman in her labour, brethren, so does a nation conceive. Through blood and agony, freedom is born. This suffering which we pass through in Jamaica now is the tossing of a country that shall bring forth a new world. There are midwives to this labour, preachers and patriots who know that love and not revenge is the meaning of mankind.

AARON

Deacon, how you could love somebody that whipping you?

DEACON SALE

The man who whips you cuts his own flesh, Aaron. For you are a piece of that man. Do not hate him. Twenty years ago, in Haiti, the slaves turned on their masters and butchered them. When the great generals of the Haitian revolution came to power, their cause was corrupted by greed. Even that great general Toussaint caught the contagion of hate.

But those that followed him, Dessalines, Christophe, from free slaves turned to insane emperors. Toussaint died in a cold tower in France, his dream ruined. Betrayed by his own generals, sold to his enemies. Do not hate, Aaron, however hard it seems. Revenge is easier than love. That is why we tell you to pray continually, for God delivers us from evil and from hatred in the end. And now, in honour of our absent brother Pompey, who is secretly spreading the gospel of peace over Jamaica, up in the mountains, in secret gullies, let us sing the hymn "There Were Ninety and Nine," starting at the last verse but one . . .

(He sings.)

Lord, whence are those blood drops all the way
That mark out the mountain track.

SLAVES (Singing softly.)

Lord, whence are those blood drops all the way
That mark out the mountain track.
They were shed for one who had gone astray.

DEACON SALE

Pray for Brother Pompey, scattering pamphlets of peace . . .

SLAVES (Singing.)

Ere the shepherd could bring him back.
(Shots in the distance.)
Lord, whence are thine hands so rent and torn,

They were pierced tonight with many a thorn,
They were pierced tonight with many a thorn ...
   (POMPEY *sneaks in quickly.*)
But all through the mountains, thunder riven,
And up through the rocky steep ...
   (POMPEY *hides among the crowd.*)
There arose a cry from ...

   (*Enter* SERGEANT, SOLDIERS.)

SERGEANT

Quiet! All right, all right, here we are again, Deacon. Now don't mind me, Deacon, I'd just like this little illegal meeting to stand still and be normal. It's a tune I always like meself, but don't any one of you protestants move. We're looking for a little fellow, name of Pompey, who's been preaching riot round the compounds. Now, where was we, Deacon? The last verse, I believe ... (*Sings*). *But all through the mountains.* Go on from there ... And keep the muskets cocked, men ... *Sing!*

SLAVES (*Feebly*)

But all through the mountains, thunder riven,
And up through the rocky steep,
There arose a cry from the gate of heaven,

   (SERGEANT *spots* POMPEY.)

SERGEANT

There's the black sheep we're looking for! Hold him!

SLAVES (*Loudly*)

Rejoice, I have found my sheep.
And the angels echoed around the throne,
Rejoice for the Lord brings back his own,
Rejoice for the Lord brings back his own.

(POMPEY *is held, struggles, is clubbed.*)

DEACON SALE

You've killed him, Sergeant, there's a law against this.

SERGEANT

Resisting arrest and inciting violence. Deacon,
I can't fight the law, can I? I got a call same as you,
And mine was protecting the interests of justice.
Now herd them along, you're all heading for court.
I didn't mean to do him half the damage he invited.

(*All are almost offstage when* POMPEY *rises.*)

POMPEY

Ay! you there, Sergeant. Look, Pompey resurrected!

SERGEANT

Come on, after him!

(General confusion: whistles, shots, blackout.)

Scene 15

Jamaica. GEORGE WILLIAM GORDON, *rehearsing a speech which he reads from.*

(ELIJAH, *a servant, enters.*)

ELIJAH

Mr. Gordon, Mr. Gordon, we're ready to leave now.

GORDON

I'll be down in a moment.
Your Excellency, gentlemen of this assembly, fellow
   Jamaicans,
In the history of nations, the birth of their spirit,
There can be no last battle. For the history of man
Is continual conflict, with himself, with his enemies.
The potential of a country is the mass of its people.
That torrent may be poisoned by the discolouring intellect
Of ambitious conquerors, and the blame is theirs.
Your Excellency suggests patience, to be satisfied with
   progress,
The evolution of our society, the dissolution of prejudice,
But human truths cannot be concealed in a pact.
The history of these islands has been tragic from birth,
Their soils have been scoured, their peoples forgotten,

While the powers of Europe struggled for possession.
And when that wealth has been drained, we have been
   abandoned.

ELIJAH

Your horse is ready, Mr. Gordon.

GORDON

        I am coming down. Gentlemen,
I am not satisfied with the form of the constitution.
This may flout the government, result in rebellion.
But I am prepared for this also, we must not be satisfied.
I risk my life for this; if we ask for these liberties.
We are seeking what is natural.

ELIJAH

        Mr. Gordon, you going be late, suh.
Dem have plenty people gathering round the courthouse.
And is a long ride to Kingston. You best come now.

GORDON

If one last battle, which remains to be fought,
Means the absolute freedom of those who have suffered
With patience, faith, and humour, I shall incite that battle.
I am compelled, at the risk of hanging for that truth,
To tell this country, and these islands, the meaning of liberty:
That it must be fought for, regardless of its price.
Does it sound good to you, Elijah?

ELIJAH

Sound good enough, sir,

For them to put a rope round your neck.
Come, sir, Kingston.

GORDON

And certain execution.

(*He exits.*)

Scene 16

On one side of the stage, enter POMPEY. *He carries a breadfruit and a dented bugle. On the other side,* CALICO *enters. Both are grimy.*

POMPEY

What a blow this sergeant deal me on me crown! I been in flight for six days now, through hill and gully, trying to reach the rebel Maroon camp in the mountains behind God's back. It must be somewhere 'bout here, though since the rifle butt daze me, I can't read no map. I like a black, lost sheep, and hungry.

CALICO

O Lord, what's going to happen now? The bottom fell out of the sugar market. I'm ruined, all I have in my pocket is this heirloom of a golden Spanish coin. I'm ruined, that's the truth. I wish I could find Yette now, but I hear she's joined the Maroons. Some fellow called Mano, or something. Oh, what's the use. Mano, Mano, what a name for a general. Why, it could be anybody. I'm ruined.

POMPEY

How a man could have a name so anyhow, Mano? Mano whom, Mano what? I best give a blast on the bugle, this bush full of enemies. Oh God, I eh even got breath for that yet.

CALICO

I'd better get out of sight, there are wild slaves who make no distinction about a man's skin.

POMPEY (*Backing towards* CALICO.)
You can't trust these white fellers, like that sergeant. God, me head!

CALICO (*Backing towards* POMPEY.)
These fellows just take revenge, as if I invented history. I'd best give a shout and hoist up a white flag, if Yette will forgive me. Mano!

POMPEY

The best thing is to shout them. Mano! Mano!
      (*They turn together, then run off.*)
Oh God, is a white feller.

CALICO

Holy God, a mad slave! Oh God, help! Pardon!

POMPEY

Man, I ain't do you nothing. Oh God, beg your pardon!

(YETTE *appears with a musket.*)

YETTE

Shut up your jaws, both of you. There's British soldiers crawling through these plains.

CALICO

Yette, forgive me. The bottom fell out of the sugar market.

YETTE

Move, man!

CALICO

All I have left in my name in this coin.

POMPEY

Him was trying to kill me, I is a pacific man. I want to join General Mano.

YETTE

Shut up, I'm taking you to headquarters right away. March ahead, recruits.

(*They exit, marching ahead of her. Blackout.*)

Scene 17

*MANO's camp and field kitchen, Accompong. GENERAL YU
stirs a huge cauldron with a wooden ladle. RAM sits patching
a pair of pants. MANO, bare-chested, cleaning a musket.*

MANO

How this food coming, General Yu?

YU

Proceeding carefully, General Mano. I have included various
weeds, ingredients to concoct a new savour, fragments of
finished meat, flowers, spinach; all is one green swamp.

MANO *(Drinking.)*

What you going call it?

YU

Calaloo. Be patient, sir. I know an army travel on its
stomach. One thing lacking, though, that fruit of Captain
Bligh, breadfruit.

MANO

Don't worry about the breadfruit. The Lord will provide.

RAM

Oh God, look at this pants, nuh! Where Yette disappear
since morning?

MANO

Yette have the noon watch.

RAM

Mano, this troop going to pieces day after day, like my pants shredding into shreds. I wish to God we had a proper army with a couple cannon. Oh God, I juk me finger with the needle again. All of us is generals, but we need more support. All night I was figuring some tactics that would paralyse them British soldiers, but I can't think too calm with the wind ventilating my trousers and this kind of food that the general inventing. Now look, Napoleon himself said that . . .

YU

Better to observe the discretion of Buddha. Buddha observed that one may conquer a thousand thousand men in battle but he who conquer himself, he is the greatest victor. Please pass the rum, General.

(RAM *passes the rum.*)

MANO

Wait, like I hear a bugle.

RAM

Is only your belly crying. You only getting nervous. Is the bad food we eating, General. Now, how we going make rum? We best go back to slavery. At least you could drink. Napoleon used to drink good before war.

MANO

Napoleon said that God was on the side of the big battalions, but look where he finish. Well, General Emmanuel Mano say this, that God on the side of the right cause. Power consume itself, Ram. Your religion, my religion, and the general's religion teach us that. An old Jew long time gone teach that to my great-great-grandfather.

RAM

But, Chief, that's the way the world turn, power is the law, and we ain't nothing without an army and artillery. You think any man have a right to dead in this pants?

(*Shout off:* "*Mano!*")

MANO

Is Yette voice, but don't trust them soldiers, scatter. Hide the tureen, General.

RAM

Wait, let me get on them trousers. Wait, wait.

(*They scramble into hiding. Enter* YETTE,
CALICO, POMPEY.)

YETTE

Mano! Is Yette, I bring you more recruits. We got a Chinese cook, an East Indian tactician; now we have a preacher and a ruined planter. Attention, recruits. In about five minutes, if the Maroon commander like you, you might promote to the rank of generals, for that's the way things devise here, equal powers. (MANO *and the others emerge*.) Your commander, Emmanuel Mano, sometimes known as Cudjoe, sometimes John Orr, sometimes Fédon, and various multicoloured aliases. They call he Calico; all he have left in his name is an antique Spanish coin that ain't worth much. And you there, put down the breadfruit and salute.

MANO

Your first military action, pardner, is to dedicate this fruit to today's supplies. Hand it over to General Yu.

YU

Just in time, General, nice fruit just good for pot.

MANO

What's your Christian name, and what make you fight for the cause of emancipation and constitutional progress?

POMPEY

You never heard of me?

RAM

You is a soldier?

POMPEY

I is a calypsoldier. I bugles, I incites violence, I tread the burning zones of Arabia. I was a meek and mild nigger, a pacific man, but now . . .

MANO

All right, all right, and you, Mr. Calico, hand over the coin to the auditor, General Ram. Yette, you see anything, gal?

CALICO

General, this is an ancestral heirloom, my great-grandfather found it and died with it as Jeremy Ford when he searched for Guiana with Sir Walter Raleigh.

MANO (*Shouting impatiently.*)

Well, ain't it an Indian you giving it to, and ain't it an Indian them did want it from? Boy, pass the subscription before I chop off your brains.

YU

Food cook will please sit and serve. I will stand watch.

POMPEY

Inform me of my duties and watch me charge the foe.

MANO

You ent too mind if we eat a little food first. Now you, what you want?

(*They sit to eat.* YU *passes plates of food around.*)

CALICO

General, the bottom fell out of the sugar market, but more than that economic fact, I was pursuing your career with interest. I hear how you have developed an army of free men. You could shoot me if you need to, but since the hand of ruin withered my crops, poverty has taught me compassion.

MANO

Friend Calico, nobody hate nobody here. I know what concern you have for the land, and you may have a proprietary right, for all I know, as you was here first . . .

CALICO

Yes, but I didn't care sufficient about those who worked it.

MANO

I say it don't matter, sometimes the times so bad a man don't have time to think properly. Now, ladle out a soup for yourself.

CALICO

I don't like Chinese food.

MANO

Well, that's all we have here, so you best swallow your pride.

YU (*Rushing at* CALICO.)

You don't like Chinese food? A smashed head brings wisdom.

MANO

Don't attack the man, General Yu, he don't mean no wrong. Pompey, how about you?

POMPEY (*Waving his musket.*)

War! To war! They holding us in the chains of bondage, and I doesn't eat dead flesh with mortal man. Oh God, they beat poor Pompey with the rod of correction, and they cast me and my people in a dungeon with the lizard and the involved serpent.

YETTE

Hear he. Good robber talk, Pomps.

MANO

What's the news in the country now, girl?

YETTE (*Eating.*)

They hanged George William Gordon from the yardarm is what I gather, and the riots in Morant Bay bursting out like sandbox pods from the tree of Liberty . . .

POMPEY

Liberty, that's a stupid phrase, that's an abused phrase. I drowned my grandmother in a spoonful of water, I is the tawny lion of Assyria, and the rod of God is the rod of violence. I defies police and parliament, I shoe the foot of the devil so he can tread the burning marl of hell. Oh, God is a white man that crack me crown, destroy the enemy.

(*Rushes at* CALICO. RAM *and* YETTE *hold him back.*)

RAM

Pompey, pal, eat your eat and don't worry.

POMPEY

Ain't this is the man who profit from my flesh and get fat on my ignorance, ain't this is the man who fatten the land and exhaust it? O God in heaven, let me bury my cracked head in the grave, for I can't stand the din of the history of un-righteousness no more.

CALICO

All I had was a coin and I gave it to Ram.

RAM

Pompey, history not a judge, not a prophet, not a priest, and not a executioner. This man never hurt, and he ain't no more responsible for the past to his father than for the future to his son. Don't grudge, don't remember, eat.

CALICO (*Aside to* YETTE)

What is your relationship with this general, if I may ask?

YETTE

I'm a woman friend. I don't have no prejudice.

POMPEY

Prejudice! The cry of the damned fiend in the whirlwind of reason . . .

(*Again he charges* CALICO *and is again intercepted.*)

MANO

Oh God, but is hard sometimes to love one another; if he get on like a beast, bind him hand and foot. I can't have no ruction in this place. He getting on like some mad Haitian rebel. Wait, I hear the bugles of the first battalion.

(*They tie* POMPEY*'s hands and gag him.*)

RAM (*Searching.*)
The hour of battle is at hand. Where the map? Where the map I draw out with the battle tatix?

YU
Do not touch the calaloo pot.

RAM
You damn stupid Chinaman, look how you tear up me map. What you know about war?

YU
Is better always to make soup than war.

RAM
This the map I spent all last night designing.

YU
Short of paper. Map was entirely without tactical value. Hence used to start fire.

MANO
Yette, bring the military list. Loose Pompey, and make him stop whining there as a mongrel dog. Boy, whether you

like it or not, we uniting against this oncoming British platoon. Take away the tureen, General Yu.

YETTE

General Yu, where the military list? It was in your coat there last night.

MANO

Oh God, when West Indians going learn discipline, much less the art of war?

POMPEY (*Singing.*)
The drums and colours come, and the canes marching to
war.

YETTE

Here the list, General Mano.

MANO

Ram, run up to the rock and signal for me.

RAM

Right.
(*He runs off.*)

POMPEY (*Singing.*)
The drums and colours come to defeat us as before . . .

MANO

All right, we going into council. General Yu, you keep
    watch ahead;
Ram signal the rebels across the ravine that we ready.
(*Reads.*)
One pair washikongs, two pairs shirts, one underwear, two
parts scallion, one part fried rice . . . Give me patience;
Christ, this is the laundry list . . .

POMPEY (*Singing and marching.*)
The conqueror that leads us into war,
Oh, the conqueror that leads us into war.

MANO

It have the Royal Welsh Fusiliers, and the Black
Watch . . . Hey, Ram, what is this Black Watch, coloured
boys?

CALICO

It's a regimental description . . .

MANO

Now General Yu report! Hurry up, hurry up! Don't bother
bow.

YU (*Bowing profusely.*)
As special cook for British regiments from Newcastle to the
northern plain, have fixed company meals thus. Placing

many haphazard ingredients into Chinese special Friday-
night menu, into vast cauldron of polluted soup, last night
whole company complain of interior disorder, but during
supper several green British soldiers demand more, kicking
this person in the shin . . .

POMPEY

Oh God, they coming for Pompey, hide me, hide me . . .

YETTE

Take it easy, boy!

RAM (*From above.*)

I can see the sunlight winking on their muskets and the
sergeant have a broad and blond mustache . . .

POMPEY

Oh God, the sergeant, the sergeant.

YU

This same platoon should be considerably weakened by
dysentery, yet compelled to march. I remember the advice
of General Ram, that an army travel on its stomach.

MANO

Yette, you going be in the vanguard and conduct this
interesting flank movement. When the regiment passing
between this gully of the dried riverbed, sick and helpless

and ready to die . . . then you suddenly appearing like a mirage of woman and water onto the parched plain, without musket, singing a local song, and then display a vulnerable flank. Show me the artillery.

YETTE *(Showing a leg.)*

So?

YU

Naturally, men sick and tired will stop and whistle. Sex being a great republic . . .

YETTE

Mano is British not French soldiers, you think they going look?
Them fellers well trained in discipline.

MANO

They bound to look.

YU

We lashing into them.

MANO

Then Ram, at some point, you getting up slowly and making off-break remarks about the regimental British cricket team, then I giving the other band a signal, and we lashing into them with stone, ladle, iron. This one musket I giving to Pompey so he can shoot the sergeant.

POMPEY (*Grabbing a musket.*)

The sergeant, the sergeant!

RAM (*Waving frantically above.*)

Boys, boys, clear the road, clear the road, they coming . . . !

POMPEY

Oh God, revengement is mine. Come, Brother Calico!

(POMPEY *and* CALICO *exit.*)

MANO (*To* YETTE)

But let me tell you, woman. You best not act this part too good or is blows in your skin, and your regimental colours going be black and blue . . .

YETTE

Don't mind that, scatter, scatter!
(*She sits singing as the regiment comes on.*)
Fan me, soldier man, fan me.
Fan me, soldier man, fan me.
Fan me, soldier man, fan me, oh
Gal, your character gone.

SOLDIER (*Shouts.*)

I'll see you later, sausage!

(*The* CAPTAIN *blows a whistle; all halt.*)

CAPTAIN

Halt! stop that drumming.
Sergeant, find out who shouted to that woman,
I'm sick of this indiscipline.

SERGEANT (*Moving among* SOLDIERS.)

The young captain is very thirsty, mates, and he would like
me to know which of you poor suffering buggers, sweating
on the march all day and fighting in a rebellion which you
really have no faith in, cried out, I'll see you later, sausage, or
various innocent words to that effect, thereby slandering this
lady's physique. Purdy? Williams? Fairweather? Matheson?
No answer, Captain, they never even seen her before.

CAPTAIN

You there! strumpet! Ease there on your muskets.

YETTE

Is it me, my blue-eyed captain?

CAPTAIN

Is there a river near here?

YETTE (*Singing.*)

Oh, down by the river, he gave me his word,
I'll be back tomorrow is all I heard.
Oh, now he's gone, and he rots in the sun . . .
There's river through the canes to your right, Captain Blue-
eyes.

POMPEY

You see how she flirting? (*He rises.*) Surrender in the name of General Mano, defender of freedom, or is stones in your skin.

CAPTAIN

Shoot that fellow, Sergeant, he's a runaway slave.

POMPEY

You can't shoot me.

CAPTAIN

Present your musket.

POMPEY

I ain't have no damn rifle.

CAPTAIN

Prime locks.

POMPEY

All you best surrender.

CAPTAIN

Fire!

(*They wound* POMPEY.)

Come on, men, after them.

(MANO's *army battles with the* SOLDIERS.)

YETTE (*Singing above the chaos.*)
Oh, the soldier he leads a terrible life,
The soldier he leads such a terrible life,
He fights for man's folly, confused by each cause,
And the captain prohibits his preference for . . .

(*The* SOLDIERS *are beaten off.*)

RAM

They killed the boys this time. General, we can't keep fighting them like this, it ain't make sense. Look how they kill Pompey.

YETTE (*Moving in the field.*)
He fights for man's freedom, confused by a cause.
And the captain prohibits . . .
Oh, they killed my blue-eyed captain.

MANO

How you feeling, Pomps?

POMPEY

I feel cold in the heart, General.
I think the chief calling Pompey. He shoot me in a bad place, that feller.

MANO

Yette, get the man some water. I think Pompey grievous hurt.

POMPEY

Nigh unto death, as it say in the Book. Nigh unto death.
How is so dark and so cold? Ain't it noontime?

MANO

Cheer up, Pomps, we has great things to do yet in the name
of freedom.

POMPEY

I dead tired, Mano. I can't fight no more. We lose, is no use
   fighting.
Freedom will never come.

MANO

Look your friend Calico, Corporal.

POMPEY

I ain't no corporal, Mano, a feller give me this uniform. You
think we going win, Mano?

MANO

We was born free in the sight of the Lord, and the Lord
won't close his eye because the sun sink. One day, praise
God, the freedom we was born with bound to come. See,
your friend Calico here . . .

POMPEY

Calico, it have white fellers what dead down there. But they
was soldiers. I spoil everything. I ruined the attack because I
am a fool since I born.

CALICO

Everybody makes mistakes.

POMPEY

We all the same in the dark. We all in the same descending
darkness. I ain't know what to tell you, Calico.

YETTE

Pompey. Drink some water.

(*A trumpet blows retreat.*)

POMPEY

That's a nice-sounding bugle. But is dark, eh? Where
Ram?

MANO

Ram.

RAM

I here with you, Pomps.

POMPEY

Hello dere, you old coolie. You crying or what?

RAM

Bear up, Pomps; don't give up yet.

POMPEY

It ain't water I want, Yette. I want all you boys stick together, you hear? All you stick together and don't hate nobody for what they is or what they do. This is all we land, all we country, and let we live in peace. I want all you hold hands there near me, and live like brothers. Calico, don't 'buse coolie, and coolie don't 'buse Mano, and, Mano, give the boys a break sometimes, because this is confusion time.

(*He dies. Trumpet.*)

RAM

They sending back a burial detail. We best get out.

YETTE

Where will they bury my blue-eyed captain, I wonder.

(*More shots.*)

MANO

If you don't haul you tail out of here, they'll bury you alongside your blue-eyed captain. Come on, Ram, we'll come back for Pompey.

(*All exit running, except* YETTE.)

YETTE

I could open a store with the pickings of dead soldiers' pockets. (*She picks up a badge.*) It's only a bloody badge for valour, no use to a woman.

(*Enter* SERGEANT *with* PATROL.)

SERGEANT

Burial detail, halt! You still here?

YETTE

Woman's work is never done, Sergeant. We clean up.

SERGEANT

You know we should have shot you right away, when you
    begun it,
Hiking up your flank and perturbing the regiment.
What yer waiting for, get on and bury them all
Or heap them in the cart!

(*The* SOLDIERS *gather the dead.*)

YETTE

His eye is on the sparrow, Sergeant, it wasn't me.
It was your imagination that started the battle.

SERGEANT

Robbing the dead, what a ghoulish occupation.

YETTE

And there goes the lovely drummer boy.

SERGEANT

You women cause all the trouble.

(YETTE *laughs.*)

What are you doing in such a rum game, girl?
You're not with them, are you? I mean those fellows.
Seems a girl like you could live in a great mansion.

YETTE

I had that once, Sergeant, but it didn't come to much.
You know, you find what's honest and you live by that.
Are you happy in your trade yourself, then?

SERGEANT

I never thought much about it till you asked me.
Seen many dead in many parts of all the empire, but
As you were singing, the soldier's life is hard.
Are you with that fellow, what's his name?

YETTE

                    Emmanuel Mano.
I'm with nobody, Sergeant. Man is a beast. Move your
foot.

SERGEANT

What are you looking for?

YETTE

                    I found it, it's a Spanish coin.
It belongs to a friend of mine that's ruined.

(*A* SOLDIER *comes up.*)

SOLDIER

We're ready to move on now, Sergeant.

SERGEANT

You go on ahead, Corporal. A coin?

YETTE (*Holding up the coin.*)

It's been worn and rubbed and abused, worn shiny
Like some of the good women in the world. Make a good
   chain, though.
Oh, look at poor Pompey, left alone in the dimming field.
Good night, poor sergeant.

SERGEANT

There's the bugler. Why poor?
I'd as soon be back home, cold as it is at this time o' year,
And not conquering the heathen but defending me own
   hearth.
I had nothing against the little fellow, but my job.
And that I can't think about. I'm sure you'll win, though.
There's many in England and all over the world
Who wish you the best. Good dusk to you, then. March!

(*Exit* PATROL *to slow drum.*)

EPILOGUE

Night: The field. Enter MANO, YETTE, RAM, CALICO,
GENERAL YU *looking for the body of* POMPEY.

MANO

All you fan over this field, but watch out for soldiers.

This Pompey so troublesome, you can't find him when he
    dead,

Like he misplace his own corpse? Anybody see him?

YETTE

See him here, Commander, serious as a stone. Ram, the spade,

This have to be one rapid burial, and don't make no noise.

RAM

A man supposed to be buried sitting up, in my religion.

YU *(Holding the body.)*

Nonsense, burning the body is custom, then scatter ashes

Of this salt of the earth, as the wind shall see fit.

RAM

Leggo, leggo the body, you foolish Chineeman. I say
    leggo . . .

CALICO

But anyone know what religion Pompey practised?

MANO

Pompey was an everythingist, now he is a nowherian.
But too much contention, we giving him general burial.
Lord, can't a man even get a good rest when he dead?

YETTE

Well then, blow the bugle faintly, and, Mano, say some
    words.

MANO

Kneel in your own peculiar fashion, enough of the
    wrangling.
All the nations of this earth is compounded in one man.

YETTE

Don't shout, man, the soldiers.

(*They all kneel.*)

MANO

                I going say all that I can quick.
In the name of the Father, Son, and Holy Ghost;

In the name of Tamoussi, Siva, Buddha, Mahomet,
   Abraham,
And the multitude of names for the eternal God,
Amen. O God, this dust was once mankind and none will
   listen,
We are gathered together, before whose eyes there is no
   night,
To bury one significant fragment of this earth, no hero,
But Pompey . . . Corporal Pompey, the hotheaded
   shoemaker.
But Pompey was as good as any hero that pass in history,
For this is the hinge on which great nations revolve,
For Pompey's squingy eyes perceived the salvation,
Which Thou preparedst in the presence of our
   enemies,
Before the face of all people . . .

RAM

Hurry up, hurry up.

MANO

Before Calico people, and General Yu people, and
Before Yette kin, and Ram generation. Now you all.

(*They file past the corpse.*)

YETTE

I remember him pinching my flank and stealing the
   supplies.

RAM

I remember him who loved peace, compelled to play soldier.

CALICO

I remember how he forgave me, though I didn't do him
  nothing.

MANO

General Yu?

YU

Remember he couldn't eat, heart full of sorrow.

RAM

What happen now, you done?

MANO

Put this dust back in the earth.

(*They lower the body through the trapdoor.*)

YETTE

Bury him with the coin that Calico gave him.

MANO

Fling it to hell, into darkness and oblivion, for this is the
enemy that bring man into division. Look, it mark "In God
We Trust," but a man face carved on it.

(*He tries to get the coin from* YETTE.)

YETTE

Mano, this is only a symbol. It not evil in itself. And it have its good uses, if power won't abuse it. Think, Mano, you ain't never going to be so rich as to know how strong it is.

MANO

Is only sometimes I can't bear our history, our poverty, and the wrangling of them fellers. And we part of the world, girl? What we could do without power?

RAM

We only a poor barefoot nation, small, a sprinkling of islands, with a canoe navy, a John Crow air force, and a fête father philosophy, but in the past we was forged, Mano, and, oh, I can't talk enough to tell you, but for this Pompey dead, stupid as he did seem. I wish I could talk. Oh, where the feller with the language to explain to this man?

YETTE

All you taking this too serious, is only a play.
Pompey boy, get off the ground, before you catch cold.

RAM

I ain't like the way he quiet, yes?

YETTE

Shout in his ear, that the emancipation going come,
That the bells going ring out, and a new age begin. Pompey!
You holding up the works.

(*The bells start ringing.*)
Oh God, the battle won, the emancipation beginning.

RAM

You mean all the history of our past going fuss over one man?
A poorakey shoemaker who can't even act good?

(CROWD *comes on, curious.*)

POMPEY (*Suddenly jumping up.*)
Who the hell can't act good, and who you calling poorakey?
And how is emancipation, today is federation.
You there, Sergeant, you had no right to hit me so hard.
(*He runs among the* CROWD.)

MANO

Lord, trouble again, trouble again. Thank God the little men of this world will never keep still.

(*The* CHORUS *appears above.*)

POMPEY

How you mean, man? The man nearly mash up me memory.
But I feel it coming back.

CHORUS

That web Columbus shuttled took its weave,
Skein over skein to knit this various race,

Though warring elements of the past compounded
To coin our brotherhood in this little place.
And now, Time's steward, memory, hoists his mace,
Quadrado's ghosts whirl backwards in a wind,
The foam laurels those sailors fished so deep,
Those marching men, those horns and seas we sounded,
That all night long split the unquiet sky,
Faint, in the dim shell of the echoing mind,
And the past turns to its forgetful sleep.
Return again, where buried actions lie,
For time is such, alternate joy and pain,
Those dead I raised have left us vows to keep.
Look, a new age breaks in the east again.

(*Lights full up. Quatro music.* MASKERS *dance down steps
and up aisles.*)

POMPEY (*Leading the carnival.*)
So, you men of every creed and class,
We know you is brothers, when you playing Mass,
White dance with black, black with Indian, but long time
Was rebellion,
No matter what your colour, now is steel and drums.
We dancing together with open arms.
Look on our stage now and you going see
The happiness of a new country
When it was:

CROWD

*Bend the angle on them is to blow them down, is to blow them
down.*

*Bend the angle on them is to blow them down, is to blow them
down.*

When the bayonet charge is the rod of correction.

*Shout it everyone, when the bayonet charge is the rod of
correction,*

Full rebellion.

(*All go out dancing except* POMPEY.)

POMPEY

Mano, Ram, Yu, Yette, wait for me, wait for me.

Don't leave me behind, the most important man in this
country!

(*Carnival music.*)

(*Fade-out.*)

THE HAITIAN EARTH

The play was produced on the Morne, Castries, St. Lucia, by the government of St. Lucia on August 1–5, 1984, to commemorate the 150th anniversary of Emancipation. Directed by Derek Walcott. Set design was by Richard Montgomery, costumes by Sally Montgomery. The cast, in order of appearance, was as follows:

DESSALINES—*Gandolph St. Clair*

BOAR—*Anthony Lamontagne*

CHORUS—*Sixtus Jeanne Charles*

BARONESS—*Caroline McNamara*

ANTON—*Jon Clitter*

TOUSSAINT—*Arthur Jacobs*

MATRON—*Julia Bird*

CALIXTE-BREDA—*Bernard Mogal*

BARON—*David Frank*

CLERK—*Dunstan Fontenelle*

PROPRIETOR—*Irvin Norville*

STUDENT—*Irvin John*

VASTEY—*John Vitalis*

CHRISTOPHE—*McDonald Dixon*

MARIE-LOUISE—*Hermia Norton-Anthony*

DRIVER—*Irvin Norville*

YETTE—*Norline Metivier*

POMPEY—*Augustin Compton*

ANGELLE—*Anne Daniel*

BOUKMANN—*Eric Branford*

BIASSOU—*Irvin Norville*

MOISE—*George "Fish" Alphonse*

SERGEANT—*Dunstan Fontenelle*

OGÉ—*Malcolm Alexander*

CHAVANNES—*Ricardo Didier*

LECLERC—*Yves Roques*

PAULINE—*Caroline McNamara*

SECRETARY—*David Frank*

CAST OF CHARACTERS

JOHN JACQUES DESSALINES, *a slave, then first Emperor of Haiti*

THE CHORUS, *a peasant woman in martial costume*

A BARON, *a visitor to Haiti*

BARONESS DE ROUVRAY

CALIXTE-BREDA, *owner of the Breda plantation*

ANTON CALIXTE, *illegitimate son of Calixte-Breda*

TOUSSAINT L'OUVERTURE, *Calixte-Breda's coachman; afterwards a commander of the Haitian Army*

A PROPRIETOR

A STUDENT

VASTEY, *secretary to Christophe*

HENRI CHRISTOPHE, *a waiter; later a general; then King of Haiti*

MARIE-LOUISE, *his wife*

A PRIEST

YETTE, *a mulattress*

POMPEY, *a slave; later heir to the Breda plantation*

ANGELLE, *a slave*

BOUKMANN, *a slave leader of the revolt*

BIASSOU, *a slave general*

MOISE, *slave nephew of Toussaint; afterwards a general*

A SERGEANT

OGÉ AND MULATTO DELEGATES TO THE FRENCH ASSEMBLY

CHAVANNES

GENERAL LECLERC, *Napoleon's commander in Haiti*

PAULINE LECLERC, *his wife*

A SECRETARY TO LECLERC

ACT I

Scene 1

Dawn. The sound of hungry cattle, a small herd, in the
darkness, and in between, the sound of the sea. San Domingo.
A wide, wild beach.
DESSALINES, *as a* boucanier *(buccaneer), a dirty rag*
around his forehead, a jacket of untanned leather, animal
skin for sandals, is turning a carcass of wild meat on a spit.
A huge boar lumbers up among a shale of rocks, fierce-eyed,
slavering, with long white tusks.

DESSALINES

Venir! Venir, salaud!
    (*He withdraws a knife and walks towards the boar, which*
        cowers, its tusks bared, its lips snarled back.)
Hai!
    (*The boar charges.* DESSALINES *leaps aside and falls as the*
boar spins around and charges again, its tusk ripping his calf.
The boar wheels again and stands, watching. DESSALINES,
eyes wide open in angry astonishment, rubs his lacerated calf

and shakes a bloody finger at the animal. He talks to it softly
in Creole.)

You come here, you see me minding my cows,
Trying to make a life, you black like me,
And now you cut me. I do you anything?
Eh?

(He walks towards the boar.)

Now the Frenchmen will come here, and they will see
That they had a nigger here, and I won't be able to run fast
Because you cut me, you, a nigger like myself. Eh! Eh!
(The boar lunges again and DESSALINES *lets out a scream*
that rips the whole beach as he and the boar tangle in the
sand, man and animal grunting and honking in the spraying
sand. DESSALINES *cuts the boar's throat. He wipes the blood*
on his mouth.)

I had this wild dream that I would kill a boar.
I had it sleeping on this wild beach last night.
I'll tell you, *cochon,* the sea frothed like your mouth.
And I have magic in me, and power, to kill the sea.

(The boar, dying, grunting in death spasms, stretches out.
Still.)

My friend, I think God send you as a sign.
Nothing can kill me. My name is Dessalines.
Jean Jacques Dessalines. Nothing can kill me.
(He looks around, sees the wide empty beach, the herd of wild
cattle. The lonely desolation of it all. He shouts. There is no
echo because of the sea. He shouts louder. He shouts again.)
You all can have it! I don't want it.
Take it! Take all of it!

I will drive the French pigs into that sea,
And when I come back here, on this same beach,
I not going to look like this.
The next time you see me, I will be a king!
The hills, the sea, will echo with my name.
DESSALINES! DESSALINES!

    (*His figure recedes down the wild beach. Music begins.*)

CHORUS

L'heure la couronne fumée,
Ka monter la montagne
Oui ça i ka chanter?

CHORUS OF PEASANTS

Toussaint!
Toussaint!

CHORUS

Et l'heure tonnère, en ciel,
Ka secouer nos collines,
Et l'éclair fait un signe,
Oui moune nous ka songer?

CHORUS OF PEASANTS

Dessalines!
Dessalines!

CHORUS

When that big drum,
The thunder shake Haiti,
When we see the
Lightning flash his signal,
What man we does remember?

CHORUS OF PEASANTS

Christophe! Henri Christophe!

(DESSALINES *nods to the mounted* SOLDIERS. *Confidently*
he moves to the front of the group and chains himself.)

Scene 2

Noon. The long, hot road. The SLAVES; DESSALINES, *lost*
among them, walking, receding. Dust. They pass Belle Maison,
the Calixte-Breda mansion. Some miles out of Le Cap.
A garden. ANTON, *a young mulatto, watching a group of*
SLAVES. *A young white woman, the* BARONESS, *finely*
dressed, is coming towards him. He waits. The BARONESS
draws alongside the young man. They watch the group.

BARONESS

Who are they?

ANTON

Who? . . . They're slaves,
Baroness.

BARONESS (*Affectionately*)

Idiot, I know that. I mean
Where are they going?

ANTON

To the spectacle, I imagine.
You'll see them tomorrow.

BARONESS

They looked quite happy.

ANTON

It's a break for them.

BARONESS

You look upset. Isn't this a common sight?

ANTON

In a time when the reek of massacre
Is on every napkin, when the stench of sweat
Floats over the dinner linen from the compounds,
I'm tempted to write out my thoughts, but thought
Is like a thicket without a clearing,
And I begin, then my wrist is paralysed.
I look at my hand and I abhor my own colour;
It is mixed, a compound, like the colour of the earth.
And I put my pen aside, and I live apart
From thought. I have read all of them,
Rousseau, Voltaire, but it is as if I'm not entitled

To thought, to ideas. Entitlement, entitlement,
Enlightenment, enlightenment. White
Is the colour of thought, black of action.
And I'm paralysed, madame, between thought and
    action.
Perhaps I should not be a writer but a soldier.
Perhaps I should be there with them. A bastard.

                BARONESS

Perhaps it's that which I find so attractive.

                ANTON

Perhaps I'm very tired of Western culture
And its privilege of ideas, perhaps,
Except for art, I see the whole technological
Experience as failure, but true or not,
I have no wish to go back to the bush.
I think their African nostalgia is rubbish.
But I'm not going to be drawn in by a drawing room.
No doubt, Baroness, you think I must either hate it
Or envy it, which amount to the same.
I must think of these things.

                BARONESS

        Why, dear boy?

                ANTON

Because I'm a bastard, a mulatto,
A man without rights.

(DESSALINES, *walking, has moved up to the front, nearer the*
SOLDIERS. *He whistles happily. He gets nearer to a young*
slave, JACKO, *who is manacled by the neck to one of the*
SOLDIERS' *horses.*)

DESSALINES

You still troublesome, Jacko?

(JACKO *turns his head.*)

JACKO

Dessalines? What you doing here, my man?

DESSALINES

You shut your arse, nigger. *Paix chou'ous, garçon!*

JACKO

They say you was dead. They say they burn you.

DESSALINES

Black magic, boy. Black magic. Keep walking.
What could be safer than this? Don't worry.
Tonight you'll be free. I'm walking to my throne.

SOLDIER

No disorder there. You! Fall back!

(*The* SOLDIER *yanks* JACKO *forward and starts trotting his*
horse so that JACKO *has to trot.* DESSALINES *laughs, shouts.*)

DESSALINES

Courir! Courir! Run, nigger, run,
I betting on you.

(*Some of the* SLAVES *join in the laughter.* DESSALINES*'s
expression changes slowly. Down the road, the* SOLDIER
galloping, and JACKO, *trying to keep up, is dragged for some
length in the dirt.*
ANTON *and the* BARONESS. TOUSSAINT *comes towards
them. He pauses. He is in coachman's livery.*)

ANTON

What is it, Toussaint? There, you saw what happened?

TOUSSAINT

Perhaps he deserved it. The carriage.
How many will there be to go to Le Cap?

ANTON

All of us. Harness four. Wait. Toussaint . . . You do not have
to go. You know that?

TOUSSAINT

Four. *Excusez moi, madame, m'sieu.*

(TOUSSAINT *bows. The* BARON, ANTON, *the* BARONESS,
M. CALIXTE-BREDA, *a matronly* WOMAN.)

CALIXTE-BREDA

Mirabeau, Robespierre, Rousseau, Voltaire,
What are all these metropolitan names, Baron?
They're romantics overcome by the odour of the mob.

MATRON

Bouquet d'Afrique.
                    (*The guests laugh.*)
A man's origins hides in his linen.

(*More laughter.*)

CALIXTE-BREDA

And this man . . . Ogé . . . He's a mulatto.
He was a member of the Friends of the Negro . . .
He is, was, my son Anton's very good friend.

BARON

Was? He isn't dead yet. That's tomorrow, no?

CALIXTE-BREDA

He's as good as dead. Maybe just as well.
Rights for the mulattos today means rights
For the slaves tomorrow. Well, there's damned
Little entertainment here apart from executions.

MATRON

I had a surly cook once. Very rude. Finally,
Desolated, I threw him into the oven.

(*Laughter.*)

That was after my husband died.
No. It's true. Don't be shocked, Baron.
It is funny now I come to think of it.

CALIXTE-BREDA

Their trial has lasted two months. It has been fair.
They began an insurrection. Chavannes killed my friends.
I have no feeling of revenge. You must write that
In your esteemed style, Baron.
You must see that Anton, my adopted son,
Is a mulatto. But I treat him like my own.
So we aren't all that cruel.

MATRON

You should display more gratitude, Anton.

(CHORUS *enters, marching at funeral step, to a single*
drumbeat on her drum, CHORUS *sings.*)

CHORUS

I

C'était bel jour comme 'jourd'hui.
Eux prendre les deux mulattres:
Ogé avec Chavannes.
Eux 'taient aller Paris

En culottes et cravates
Eux pas 'taient Nègre savannes
Pour demander leur droit,
Leur droit, leur droit, mulattres.

II

Mais mulattres trop couillons,
Pis eux ni grands cabanes.
Eux croient eux c'est gens blanc
Et, Nègres ka rester cabrits
Z'animaux et moutons,
Alors jourd'hui, jourd'hui
Bon Dieu fait eux pardon
Eux prend Ogé ec Chavannes
Pour faire crucifixion.

III

Bon Dieu, toute moune c'est même
Mulattres, bechés et Nègres,
Mais nous sourds, nous aveugles
Tout n'omme eux c'est une race
Messieurs bi-dim, bam-bam
La guerre kai commencer
A' nous aller la place
A' nous La Place des Armes.

I

It was a lovely day,
A day just like this one.
They took the two mulattos

Named Ogé and Chavannes
And stretched them in the sun.
The two, they went to Paris
In trousers and in ties
To plead the mulattos' cause
Before the French Assembly,
And what they did to them
You will see, you will see!

II

These two men they were fools
Because they had good beds.
They thought that they were free,
They had a right to ask it,
Brotherhood, liberty.
They learnt good French in schools
But what was in their heads
Will roll into a basket.

III

God, all men are one race
But men are deaf and blind,
They pleaded for their case
But now their plea is wind,
Wind in the marketplace.
And Justice, she so blind!
And Justice, she so blind!

Scene 3

Night. The city of Le Cap. Crowds in the street. A carnival
atmosphere. The gang of SLAVES, DESSALINES *among*
them, being herded along to an open square, where there
is a platform and two wheels. Kettledrum rolls.
A CLERK *mounts the platform and reads, by the light*
of a torch held by a SOLDIER,
the death sentence.

CLERK

They are to be taken to the Place des Armes,
And the opposite side to that appointed
For the execution of white criminals, and
Have their arms, legs, and ribs broken
While alive, upon a . . .

(DESSALINES *sits among the gang of* SLAVES *in the square,*
watching the gibbet. The square is filling with SLAVES *from*
other estates, SOLDIERS *guarding them.*
Auberge de la Couronne. Laughter, drunken CITIZENS,
PROPRIETOR. CHRISTOPHE, *as a waiter, serving drinks to*
a table of MULATTOS *sitting apart. A* STUDENT, VASTEY
BARON. *The sound of the inn growing louder.*)

CLERK'S VOICE

Scaffold erected for that purpose, and
Placed by the executioner upon wheels,
With their faces turned towards heaven,

There to remain as long as it shall
Please God to preserve life; after
This, their heads to be severed from
Their bodies and exposed upon stakes.

PROPRIETOR

I say if it happen, it happen, and life must go on!
You know who have the pure philosophy?
These women!
  (GRACES, *three handsome, light-skinned women in*
            republican costumes.)
Our three girls, Marie, Thérèse, and Yette,
Egalité, fraternité,
So to forget the horror
A little music, and
A nous! The three Graces!

  (*The three* GRACES, YETTE *among them, dressed as*
    La Liberté. The GRACES *begin their worn routine.*
  This comprises a ballet of revolution, around a chained
                NEGRO.)

GRACES (*Singing.*)
Allons, enfants, allons, messieurs,
Le jour de gloire est arrivé.

  (*A grimy tableau on a platform. A chained half-naked*
  NEGRO; *around him the three costumed* GRACES, *holding up*
    a sign: LA LIBERTÉ DE SAINT DOMINGUE.)

YETTE (*To* STUDENT)

You working damn hard for a free coffee, *garçon*.

STUDENT

Paix chou'ous. I am an intellectual whore. I admit.

VASTEY

You taught us the art of atrocity, civilisation.
The science of massacre. There were once in this place
A million Indians. Today there are six hundred.
Their slaughter was in the interest of science?

STUDENT

I have studied philosophy in Paris itself.
I don't know why you should feel so confused.
The torture is of no consequence, here is the reason:
This is hot. This is black. There's no milk in it.
You know what coffee is? A slave is pure coffee.
But what's a mulatto like her? *Café au lait.*
I am in a café; I am a Catholic, a colonial, look.
If I mix coffee with milk, it's no longer coffee.
                    (*He indicates.*)
It is sentimental to base a civilisation
Upon a peasantry, culture is based on intellect,
On hierarchy and order, the Church herself,
The spangled, dizzying definition of angels,
Archangels, saints, canonical decrees
Admit the ascent towards that radiance

Of utter thought, for what's the Supreme Being
If not the Utmost Intellect?

YETTE

True. True.

STUDENT

                And since, in nature,
We see the evolutions of power and servitude,
How one system sharks into another's maw,
How everything is gloved in appetite
To feed the major beasts, how there is difference
Even in the affects of nature, in cities,
Blizzards; in jungles: dark rain, it follows
That there is size, and scale, and service,
And that at the bottom of the pyramid,
The apex, of every sane society, the peasant,
And lower than the peasant, the slave;
The slave, who even in his own family,
No less than the obscurest beetle,
Gives orders as the father to his spawn,
Or you might as well chuck the whole thing in a ditch
And call confusion order, and not chaos.
Saint Domingue, therefore, despite its slaves,
Remains an excellent example of natural order,
Obedience to the Church in servitude,
Protection of the slaves, its children,
Harvest, and in the New World, in terms of example,
Is more than Europe, an earthly paradise.

Even Paradise had its revolutionary angel,
And it was the first revolt, wasn't it,
That flared up that order? It was the light-bringer
That tried to make the celestial order chaos
And, out of heaven, made hell. It is for this
And not for their politics these men are punished.

(*He exits.*)

PROPRIETOR

Makes plenty sense to me. Coffee is coffee.
Coffee with milk is not coffee, but *café au lait.*
Therefore, sir, you are not a cup of coffee.

VASTEY

Don't talk to me about Paris.
You see what they do to mulattos who go to Paris . . .

BARON

That is one arrogant nigger over there. The waiter.
He was born in Saint Christopher, so
He calls himself Christophe.

(*He suddenly begins to sob, dryly. No one notices.*
CHRISTOPHE *refills the mug of rum.*)

VASTEY

Why was I born into this tribe of mongrels?
You hear them? They torture two of their people,
And they come here and get drunk.

3 1 7

(CHRISTOPHE *turns, assessing the smoky, raucous crowd.*)

CHRISTOPHE

Just now they'll start singing,
Give them enough rum, then someone
Will pull out a knife.

(*Some singing begins with the* CHORUS *of the three* GRACES.)

The nigger blood will show.
They remind me of monkeys.

VASTEY

I am one of them. Do I remind you
Of a monkey also?

CHRISTOPHE

A philosophical monkey,
Always pronouncing big words
Imported on the last boat.

VASTEY (*Rising.*)

Ape . . . you illiterate black ape!

(*Silence.* CHRISTOPHE *takes the drink and goes to the rum barrel, grins, fills the mug, and returns with it. He places it before the* BARON. *All now watch.* CHRISTOPHE *extends the napkin.*)

CHRISTOPHE

Tell me more, Excellency.

I am here to learn, mulatto.

Because the French, they know you!

They know they dealing with monkeys,

Monkeys with foulards, you don't want to be free,

You just don't want to be black. Right?

> (*He tears off the* BARON's *cravat.*)

Fat mulatto monkeys that smoke five-franc cigars

And keep bawling for more wine,

And they're killing two just now.

> (*He slaps the cigar from the* BARON's *face, pours wine onto
> his shirt. He walks up to* YETTE.)

Wouldn't it be nice if your children were white?

But making children is not a whore's business,

Any more than making revolution

Is a mulatto's.

> (YETTE *spits at him, then looks away.* CHRISTOPHE *mounts
> the platform and unchains the frightened* NEGRO, *who is
> being used for the Dance of Liberty.*)

Go. And run far.

> (*The* NEGRO *runs through the curtains and out
> of the room.* CHRISTOPHE *turns.* VASTEY *stands
> with a drawn knife.*)

Comedian.

> (VASTEY *lunges at him.* CHRISTOPHE *does not move.*
> VASTEY *pauses.*)

VASTEY

I am not an animal.

CHRISTOPHE

And those two out there, in the Place des Armes,
Ogé and Chavannes! They are animals?
Why don't you fucking cowards do something?
                    (*Suddenly, exasperated, he screams.*)
Jokers! Jokers!
They should break every one of you.
Jokers! Bloody jokers?
Wipe your nose, Baron. One day you will all have
To make up your minds if you're white or black.

(*He moves out to the street.* YETTE *leaves the stage slowly.
She enters a small room. She sits there, staring at her face in
the mirror.*)

Scene 4

Exterior: A street. Night. There is still a CROWD *in the
streets, but* SOLDIERS *among them, too, moving them on.*
CHRISTOPHE, *shirt open, barefooted, strides among them.
He meets his wife,* MARIE-LOUISE, *on the street.*)

CHRISTOPHE

Marie. You leave the baby by herself?

MARIE-LOUISE

Yes. I was just coming to look for you.

CHRISTOPHE

Know why I am in the street? I leave my work.
You want to know why?

MARIE-LOUISE

I never ask you your business.

CHRISTOPHE

Go home. Pack everything.
Henri Christophe is a waiter no more.
From tomorrow, everything will be different.
You hear me? Different! Now run home!

(MARIE-LOUISE *exits, running.* CHRISTOPHE *walks
past the band of waiting* SLAVES. *Flambeaux and
lanterns illuminate their bodies.* DESSALINES
sits up from sleeping.)

DESSALINES

They ready?

SLAVE

Almost. Soon is morning.

DESSALINES

Well, don't wake me till they ready.

(*He goes back to sleep.* CHRISTOPHE *watches him sleep.*)

CHRISTOPHE (*To* SLAVE)

How can he sleep with all this business?

SLAVE

Him? He could sleep on his grandmother grave.

(CHRISTOPHE *exits. Lights fade.*)

Scene 5

Daybreak. The same. The balcony of the Auberge de la Couronne, crowded with MULATTO WHORES. YETTE, *waving at the* CROWD. *They jeer at passersby. A gallows. The wheel. A hot, dusty square ringed by a crowd of* SLAVES, FREE COLOUREDS, *and a kind of summer pavilion for the* WHITES. TOUSSAINT, *in coachman's livery;* ANTON; *the* BARONESS, *the* BARON, CALIXTE-BREDA, *the* MATRON.

CALIXTE-BREDA

I hope the carriage is in a safe place, Toussaint.
Do you want an extra parasol, Baroness?
Ogé and Chavannes, yes. These dreamers.
They called themselves Friends of the Blacks.
I heard they offered six million in securities
To the National Debt. It's an expensive dream.
They stated in their umpteenth petition

To the Assembly: "Protestants, comedians, Jews,
The relations of criminals 'all' have their civic
Rights, but not the Mulattos." The Assembly has sworn
"Never to give rights to a bastard and degenerate race,"
So these two madmen begin a revolution.
Well, it's the end of all that stuff today.

(TOUSSAINT *unfurls a parasol over* CALIXTE-BREDA.
The WHORES, YETTE *encouraging them, scream, wave.*)

MATRON

Whores. They have no politics.

BARONESS

Please, madame. It is too hot. Shut up.

CALIXTE-BREDA

Those are our *belles de nuit.* I believe
Their sympathies are basically royalist.
She's a pretty-looking number, isn't she?

BARONESS

Their tastes are usually aristocratic.

BARON

They're the true gauge of a country's finances.
Their figures speak for themselves.
Of seven thousand mulatto women in Saint Domingue,

Five thousand are those or the mistresses of whites.
Now, isn't that prosperity?

CALIXTE-BREDA

Baron, your mind continues to bewilder me.
What value is that fact?

(*A scream, then another, rend the air. A hot, heavy silence.
The execution begins. Two* MULATTOS *exhausted from
torture.* SLAVES, *watching. Suddenly* DESSALINES
sits up.)

DESSALINES

I told you to wake me up. Shit!

ANTON

Unless all this has meaning, love
Is meaningless.
We would be animals, animals!

BARONESS

We are animals. Be a man and look.

(*There are more screams.*)

ANTON

I cannot bear this. Excuse me, gentlemen, please.
Madame Baroness, could we talk for a second?

My friends are dying. As well as pain,
Why should that sharpen and excite desire,
With me the tortured, and you the torturer?
You had me on a wheel, you broke my spirit,
You punished my presumption for loving you,
To feel my blood knotting itself in yours.
Those gasps, those screams, all those explosive spasms
Are mine there on that wheel, and you can smile,
Look at your fingernails, and go back to France,
Leaving my love to rot here in the sun,
Your soft hand melting in my hand like snow
That my own passion melted; you withdrew it,
And my hand, my heart, my life itself is empty.
I am worse than them. They died in vain.
I live in vain. Why did you encourage me?
Were you curious about what kind of beast I was,
What savageries I could invent in bed?
You cannot just smile. I beg you. Answer me.

BARONESS

Shh. Quiet! Your voice. They're praying for the dead.
As they say, "*Consummatum est.*" We consummated,
But now it's finished. I love my husband,
He is a mercilessly tolerant man. Civilised.
His civilisation bores me to death, or worse,
Bores me to certain savageries, in sweaty sheets,
But you're getting tiresome. You're making
More of a spectacle than the one here. Thank you.
Our two months here have been wonderful. Goodbye.

CALIXTE-BREDA

You will not be returning with us, then,
My dear Baron? . . . You are quite sure . . .
We're going home, Anton.

MATRON

Please stay.
We have other amusements beside this barbarity.
Saint Dominque's not such a bad place after all.

CALIXTE-BREDA

We appeal to you, sir. You need to see more
To write honestly about us. Wait, Toussaint.

MATRON

We await you, sir.
I'm sure the baroness would happily remain.

BARON

I doubt that very much, madame.
Do you wish to know my last word in this country?
I am leaving it, thank God, for good.
The more I know the men who inhabit it,
The more I congratulate myself on leaving it . . .
When one is what you planters are,
One is born to own slaves. When one is what
The greater part of these slaves are,
One is born to be a slave. Gentlemen, madame,

In this country, everybody is in his place.
I thank you all. You also, madame.

>(*He moves off, bowing.*)

CALIXTE-BREDA (*Tapping the carriage roof.*)
Allons, Toussaint. *Allons.*
Cochon. Anton!

>(ANTON *kisses the hand of the* BARONESS *and bows to the*
>BARON. *He enters the coach.*)

Let us leave quickly, something tells me that tonight
This place is going to explode.

>(*Later. Exterior. Dusk. The gibbet. The two bodies guarded*
>*by* SENTRIES.
>*From* CHRISTOPHE'*s point of view, in the middle distance,*
>*silhouetted in the dusk, there is another* BLACK, *in soiled*
>*clothes, loosely matted hair, his posture casual, almost jocular.*
>*He, too, is watching the scaffold.*
>DESSALINES. *From* DESSALINES'*s point of view:*
>CHRISTOPHE, *in waiter's uniform, paused in the center of*
>*the square.*)

DESSALINES (*Softly*)
Ay! Nègre! Ou c'est un affranchi?

CHRISTOPHE
Pardon?

DESSALINES

Ça? 'Ous pas comprendre creole?
You are a free nigger?
Behold, "A Friend of the Blacks!"
Friend of the Blacks, my arse!
The fucker owned slaves.
But if that's the way they treat
"Friends of the Blacks" after Liberty,
Equality, and Fraternity, of the great
French Republic, what will happen to
The blacks? What will happen to you?

CHRISTOPHE

Yes. I am a free.

> *(Pause.)*

> And you?

(CHRISTOPHE *moves nearer to the two bodies. There is now
a sign above them proclaiming* LES AMIS DES NOIRS.)
I cannot read. I know what the sign say.
AMIS DES NOIRS. Friends of the Blacks.
They died for all of us.

> *(He pauses, turns.)*

DESSALINES

For us? *Mulattres! Mulattres!*
Very smart yellow niggers.
They die for their own self.
What they call you, free nigger?

CHRISTOPHE

Christophe. And you . . .

(DESSALINES *has lost interest in his question. He studies the figures of the martyred men, then spits and strides away, across the square.*)

Scene 6

Night. Explosions of fire. Le Cap is burning. Smoke clouds everything. Cinders. CHRISTOPHE, *running up rickety back stairs, staggers from a cloud of smoke. He staggers again, turns, screams, blinded by smoke.*

CHRISTOPHE

Marie!
Marie-Louise!
  (*Through clearing patches of the smoke, skeletal pillars. Forms flash behind him, vague. His eyes reddened from the smoke. Utter panic. A* CHILD *is screaming.*)
Marie!
Marie-Louise!

  (*The smoke obscures his face. The* CHILD *crying. Fade-out.*)

Scene 7

Exterior. A small Catholic cemetery by a fishing village.
Coming towards us, CHRISTOPHE, MARIE-LOUISE,
a wrapped bundle.

CHRISTOPHE

Throw that thing away.
It is dead.

> (MARIE-LOUISE *shakes her head stubbornly.*)

What use is a priest?

> (*He stands watching, then steps forward for a better view. He*
> *wipes his hand across his dry mouth.*)

That's what niggers get for helping niggers.

MARIE-LOUISE

The child baptise Catholic. I want a priest.

> (PRIEST *enters.*)

PRIEST

Father, now we commit the body of this innocent to the earth from which it came, believing that for all of us there is the resurrection and the life . . . Dust to dust . . . ashes to ashes . . .

Scene 8

*Exterior day. A wagon, mule-drawn, laden with belongings,
and at the back . . .*

DRIVER

That is all you have, eh?

YETTE

All.

MAN

So, you, too?

(*The* REFUGEES, *a few mulattos among them, and even some
whites, numb, dazed. They greet the* MAN *with luggage. The
wagon moves away,* YETTE *watching.*)

YETTE

It was bad? All I save is my clothes.

MAN

Everything. I lose everything.
This is all. I had a shop. I was doing well.

YETTE

All of Le Cap burn down?

MAN (*Irritable with exhaustion*)

You remember it? You didn't see it this morning?

Well, nearly half of it burn down, you hear?

From the Auberge de la Couronne all the way

Down to the sea, flat, like a burn canefield.

My hands . . . What I am going to do with my hands?

(*He extends his palms.*)

Somebody will have to show me how to plant.

YETTE

I will have to learn, too.

(*They look towards the diminishing, rocking wagon.*)

You lose everything?

MAN

Who cares what I lose? Who cares?

When a sorrow is so big, when it is war,

Who ever think of anybody else?

Well, well, well, well, well . . .

(*He waits for the fit of despair to pass.*)

Well, well, well, well yes, well yes . . .

I have to talk to myself. To my feet.

(*He talks to his feet.*)

Come on. Let's go. Come on. Come on.

They frightened. They don't know the road.

They don't know where to go.

(*He squats.*)

Smoke, fire, and ashes. Is Sodom and Gomorrah.

All that filth and nastiness they did in there.

YETTE

But, monsieur, why they burnt it, you can say?

MAN

This city was like a woman that start off good,
Then money corrupt her and change her looks.
Once cities get too proud, God will do that.
        (*He crosses himself.*)
Today now, look at you, dirt on your cheeks,
Your laces straggling in mud? So with cities,
So with women. This city, on a Sunday morning,
With its lace balconies, its mansard bonnets,
Its church bells ringing like earrings,
And next thing, it was a whore. If you want facts,
Say the mulatto people get vex and burn it.
The wagon is coming. I'm going on that way.
And you?

YETTE

I have a little piece of land
My auntie left for me. I'll learn to plant.

(*The wagon comes, the* MAN *mounts it and waves to* YETTE.
YETTE *shoulders her belongings and climbs the hill. The*
CHORUS *enters, carrying a fork, a sack.*)

CHORUS (*Singing.*)

Alors, Yette 'trappait morceau terre,
Et i' commencait planter,

Eux deux, yeux c'est même couleur,
Terre-a, et jamette shabine,
Et pour lui-même, moi ka chanter
Et pour Christophe, Dessalines . . .
     (*Other* PEASANTS *led by* POMPEY *join her and cross the*
               stage with forks, sacks, scythes.)
So Yette find a piece of land
Where she teach herself how to plant,
Her skin the same shade as the ground,
And you'll see why I sing this chant
For her, my rose and my queen
And for Christophe and Dessalines.

          (YETTE *joins the cane cutters ahead.*)

Scene 9

Exterior. Midafternoon. The sound of a man singing in the
valley, throughout a hill slope on the mountains. YETTE,
alone on a small allotment, bent to the earth, weeding.
Uprooting rocks. A hoe on a mound beside her.

                 YETTE (*To the sky*)
. . . Papa . . . if I could write you, you would laugh now to
see your daughter, who you say would be nothing, bending
down on the earth . . . Not in a bed but in the earth,
trying to plant something. After Le Cap burn down, where
I was doing well—money, I mean—after the French
people burn down the hotel where I was working, a

man here give me a small parcel of land and I am
trying . . .

(*She takes up a gourd of calabash and drinks water, then
rests it carefully beside her and resumes her planting and
weeding. Durable, determined, teaching herself, but on the
tight edge of despair and collapse.*)

Scene 10

Exterior. Day. A field. WOMEN *from the Calixte-Breda
plantation are in a cleared cane piece, gleaning. Part of the
field is burnt black, brown, and gold.* POMPEY, *a section
overseer, stands some distance from the gleaning* WOMEN,
giving them directions. He is carrying a musket.
ANGELLE *moves from the group to a private area of the
field, in a patch of failed and yellowing corn. She is about
to enter it. She screams and staggers back. In the drying
corn a tattered black,* DESSALINES. *His eyes.*
The WOMEN *in the other parts of the field.* POMPEY *moving
towards the screaming* ANGELLE.

POMPEY

A snake? It is a snake?

WOMEN

Serpent? Serpent?

(POMPEY *running, his musket ready. The gleaning* WOMEN
draw back.)

POMPEY

Angelle! Angelle!
Restez! C'est un serpent?

(DESSALINES *rises from the corn piece. He extends both*
arms helplessly. POMPEY *aims the musket.* ANGELLE
draws back.)

DESSALINES

Wait . . .
(*He stops. Heat, silence.*)
I was just sleeping.
Is not a snake, citizen . . .
(POMPEY *listens.*)
I am on my way to the Bois Cayman.
It is over there?
(POMPEY *nods, assesses the man. His motley tattered clothes,*
the scars across his chest. The hunger, the authority.)
I am looking for a nigger they call Boukmann.
Boukmann. You know him?
(POMPEY *shakes his head no.*)
I am looking for that man, citizen.
That is all.
(*He moves past* POMPEY, *past the staring* WOMEN, *through*
the corn. On the small ridge, with its view of Belle Maison,
DESSALINES *pauses. He indicates the house.*)
Nice house. Nice house.

(*They watch his moving figure dip and disappear. The*
WOMEN *gather,* ANGELLE *among them.*)

ANGELLE

I think it was a snake.

Look, when I see him so . . .

(POMPEY *returns to the* WOMEN.)

POMPEY

Lasse parler. Assez! Mwen dis.

You never see a runaway nigger before?

Don't worry, the soldiers will get him.

Travail, travail. This damned sun making hot.

Angelle! You hear me?

(*He is drawing her into the indigo recesses of the kitchen,
among the sacks, when she sees someone and breaks
away.* POMPEY *comes to the arch of the doorway. There
is a woman there.* YETTE, *whose face we can't distinguish at
first because the light of the yard is behind her, waits. Her
hair is long but loose. She is firm-bodied, and she enters the
kitchen calmly. She carries a basket which she sets down
quietly, and dipping a cup into an open-mouthed grain
bag, she ladles out cupfuls of corn into her basket.* POMPEY
studies her.)

Who you are?

And what you doing in here?

(YETTE *continuing to ladle out the corn, silent.*)

You hear me talking to you?

You know who I am?

(*The ladling continues.* YETTE *sucks her teeth.*)

Listen, I am in charge of these provisions here.

Sacre! Answer me, woman!

(POMPEY *grabs her arm.* YETTE *stares at him. She looks
down at his gripping hand.*)

YETTE

L'agez.

Let go.

Look, mister. I'm not a thief.

(*She smashes the cup's edge against his cheek.* POMPEY *steps
back, then lunges.* YETTE *whips out a knife.*)

Eh-eh.

(*Pause. They watch each other, breathing.*)

Niggers don't fuck with me.

(*She continues ladling, picks up her basket, goes, then turns at
the arch. She extends her arm, turning it in the light
from the yard.*)

Eh! You see this colour?

Respect it. I not shamed of it.

To you, all niggers, all mulattos is whore.

And I have permission to take some corn.

From Monsieur Calixte himself.

(YETTE *exits, moving through the yard among the other*
huskers and SLAVES, *regally.* POMPEY, *fingering his cut*
cheekbone, comes to the archway. ANGELLE *comes near him.*)

ANGELLE

She cut you?

POMPEY

Yes. Who was that yellow bitch?

ANGELLE

They give her piece of land on the hill up there!
She is a mulatresse from Le Cap. A free woman.
She just come in the barracks, it have a month, now.
Her name is Yette. She don't like black people.

POMPEY

Yette.
Come on, go back to work, come on, come on.
All of you. You, too, Angelle.
      (*He hurls her back among the* HUSKERS.)
You too young to be so blasted hot!
Come on. *Faiyants!* Today the crop finish,
Tonight is fête!
  (*He moves among the* WOMEN, *slapping, shoving them, but*
    almost absently, his eyes on YETTE'*s distant figure.*)

Scene 11

Exterior. Night. The yard, a slave barbecue in the back yard
of Belle Maison. SLAVE FAMILIES *around the barbecue,*
looking out from their barrack windows. Two DRUMMERS, *a*
FIDDLER, *and a casual choir of* GIRL SLAVES. *Dancing.*
Sexual, but with self-mocking lechery.
Beyond and above them the windows of the mansion.
ANGELLE *dances,* POMPEY *moves among the crowd, hot. He*
dances a sexual parody of waltz. Laughter. He passes
TOUSSAINT *seated on a chair, a lantern at his feet, a book*
beside him. POMPEY *touches his hat. The mood of the*
chanting changes into a lament.

POMPEY

Bonsoir, Monsieur Toussaint.
It was a good crop this year, eh.

TOUSSAINT

Bonsoir, Pompey. Yes. One of the best.

POMPEY

'Ous pas kai danser? All you do is read.
Day and night, read . . .
My head. I wish I could put something in my head.
No education. That is why I am so.
You know. Woman. Good time. That's why. Dancing.
Is to make the best of this life, right, monsieur?

TOUSSAINT

Look, a new one for you.

(*Their point of view:* YETTE, *overdressed for the simple occasion, comes into the area of the firelight alone. Her clothes, her colour inhibit her. She pauses. They have turned to her. Their faces not hostile but strange. The music dwindles.*
ANGELLE *has stopped dancing. The she goes to* YETTE *and waits. They talk softly.*)

ANGELLE

We glad you come.

YETTE

Merci. I was up on the hill and I hear the
Music and I feel so . . .

(ANGELLE *puts her hand softly across* YETTE *'s lips.*)

ANGELLE

Paix! Shh . . . Is your people . . . We is neighbors now, sister.

YETTE

I too stupid to wear these clothes.
But is all I have. You see, I thought . . .
I thought the dancing was inside the house.
I bring some yams. I plant them myself.
I feel so.

(*Pause.*)

POMPEY (*Touching his face.*)
You remember this?
You are the most beautiful thing
That ever pass through here since the last full moon.
(*Pause. The others laugh.*)
Angelle, that was very nice.
She is a good girl, but she so damn hot.

YETTE
I thought it was you who was hot.

POMPEY
I hot, too.
(*He draws* ANGELLE *apart and whispers to her.* ANGELLE
nods and runs over to the MUSICIANS.)
My foot is like two yams, mulatresse.
But I can play drum, and I could sing,
I have the best voice in this valley.
And for you, I ask them to play this song.
Come dance. Or you doesn't dance with niggers?
One day you will dance in this big house.
(*The* CHORUS *joins in.* ANGELLE *claps.* POMPEY *draws*
YETTE *gently to the ring in the yard.* ANGELLE *impulsively
runs up and hugs* YETTE. POMPEY *dances.*)
Is I who write this song.
Is my own song. Now,
When you hear this song, up in that hill,

When you hear it as you planting,
You will know, down in this valley
Is Pompey singing. And I will sing,
I will sing every day, every day,
Until you get so vex you will married me.

    (*He sings his song. The* SLAVES *watching,* TOUSSAINT
                    grinning.)

Or you doesn't married niggers?

          (YETTE *laughs. They dance.*)

Scene 12

Exterior. Night. The barracks yard. A circle of SLAVES'
faces watching others dancing. Travelling behind them,
MOISE, *a fine-featured, tall young black, a bag over his
shoulder, a soft hat still dripping from rain
on the back of his head.
In another group, showing off for* YETTE, POMPEY
telling stories with excessive gestures. YETTE, *fascinated
by the obvious intensity of his approach, assessing him.
Laughter.*

YETTE

For your remembrance, in case you think I easy.
And for my own pride. I . . .

POMPEY

Yes, I know. Come on. He gone.

Scene 13

Interior. The mansion; morning streaks the windows. ANTON, *dressed for the day's work, comes down to breakfast. He senses something. He draws near the breakfast table, which is set with cutlery, crystal, excessively so, and as he draws slowly near his seat:*
He sees a white rooster, headless, and next to it a knife, folded in a napkin.

Scene 14

Exterior. A hill path, rain dripping on its green. Ochre mud. Below, the mist, the farms, TOUSSAINT *and* MOISE.

TOUSSAINT (*Embracing* MOISE.)
I will send for you . . .
When the time come.
(*He looks towards the valley. Belle Maison. A bell ringing in the field.*)
They are going to work now.
All of them. The bell.
And then the slow, melancholy shell.
(*A conch shell blows.*)
Go, then, go.

(MOISE *turns and enters the low, wet scrub, then down into the plain. Then he turns, points towards the hills.*
TOUSSAINT *nods.*)

Scene 15

Exterior. The yard. ANTON *runs across the wet yard into the stables. He has the carcass of the rooster.*)

ANTON

Toussaint!
Toussaint!
Papa!
   (CALIXTE-BREDA *appears.* ANTON *is holding the headless carcass.*)
It's here. It's here, Papa.
They started. They have started.
      (*The barracks.* SLAVES *emerge.*)
Ungrateful bastards! Bitches! Pompey, my horse!
Saddle him! I'll find that coachman. I'll find him,
And I'll roast him there!

CALIXTE-BREDA

You are under strain, Anton. You are not well.

ANTON (*To the* SLAVES)

I used to pray for you, I loved you,
I was one of you. And then this . . .
    (*To* CALIXTE-BREDA)
I'm going to the other estates.
That will teach you to love and trust niggers, sir.
And when I come back . . .

(*He circles the yard.*)
When I come back, you will tell me who . . .

(ANTON *runs off across the yard.
The* SLAVES *emerge around* CALIXTE-BREDA. *One of them
picks up the carcass and flings it into the drenched ashes.
They form a ring around him. Friendly. Two of the* WOMEN
lead him back towards the house.)

FIRST WOMAN

I know is not Toussaint. I know that.
You must believe me, Monsieur Calixte.

CALIXTE-BREDA

Marie . . . I don't know . . . I don't know, *pour vrai.*
Where is he, then? Where is he?

SLAVE

There was a man with him when we was dancing . . .

SECOND WOMAN

I know him. Everybody know him.
It is his nephew Moise.

CALIXTE-BREDA

You all are good.

FIRST WOMAN

It was not Toussaint. Try and believe that.

CALIXTE-BREDA

I hope so. Go inside. It's raining.
You will catch cold.
    (*He leaves the yard, enters the arches of the house.*)

Scene 16

*Exterior. The sky. A headless carcass of a white rooster
whirled around by* BOUKMANN. *Sound of drumming,
military.* BOUKMANN, *holding up a voodoo fetish, addressing
his* GUERRILLAS.

BOUKMANN

Entendez, Congos, Aradas, Ibos,
Entendez, Nabos, Mandingos, Haoussas!
Par là c'est les Français, ou ka 'tendre
Bangalang ces tambours-y-eux!
Maix nous mêmes, nous mêmes,
Aradas, Ibos, Congos,
Nabos, Mandingos, Haoussas!
Nous pas ni fusils, nous pas ni cannon,
Nous pas ni trompette,
We have the charms of our gods,
And we not going to die!
Personne, personne kai mourir 'jourd'hui,

No black man is going to die today!

        (He holds up his charm.)

Nous ni Vodun, nous ni Shango!

Alors, au combat! Congos,

Aradas, Ibos, Haoussas!

And if we die, even if we die,

Our souls will go back!

Back home, to Africa!

Let's go! *A'nous!*

      (BOUKMANN, *running on foot, leads the charge.*

        GUERRILLAS *descend into the plain, where*

      the FRENCH CAVALRY *advance steadily in*

      formal squares. DESSALINES, *above them,*

        watches the massacre and surprise of

          the BLACKS.)

          DESSALINES

Couillon!... Couillon!... Crazy nigger!

  (BOUKMANN, *his voodoo finery in bloody tatters, lies under*

      the dead bodies of two of his GUERRILLAS.)

        FIRST CAVALRYMAN

Boukmann! Look for Boukmann,

He's the one we want.

SECOND CAVALRYMAN

I can't tell one from the other.
They're all dead anyway. I don't know which one is his
    head.

THIRD CAVALRYMAN

Come on, that's enough. After this,
Who the hell would try again?

(*They ride off.*)

BOUKMANN

Biassou! Biassou! You dead?
Biassou! Answer!

(*Another figure rises from a heap of dead* GUERRILLAS.
BIASSOU. BOUKMANN *staggers towards him. They meet, and
together, in silence, they revolve slowly to take in the shock of
their defeat.* DESSALINES, *whistling, comes down the hill.*
BIASSOU *points and draws his sword.*)

BIASSOU

They think we finish, eh? They think so?
They will pay for this. Not just the soldiers.
Men, women, children. Their animals, their houses,
Everything. They will sweat with cowardice
At everything black.

(DESSALINES *arrives. Silence.* DESSALINES *extends
his hand.*)

DESSALINES

General Boukmann. General Biassou.
I am General Jean Jacques Dessalines.

BOUKMANN

General? Where's your army?

DESSALINES

Where's yours?
Never mind. *Pas la peine,* messieurs.
So far, I know nothing about the art of war,
But I know plenty about the art of revenge,
And I'm here to teach you niggers
A few simple tricks.
(BOUKMANN *and* BIASSOU *study him.
DESSALINES smiles.*)
Lesson one. For the time being, messieurs,
There is no God. Not black, not white.
Don't trust any of them. Can you say it?
Pour a present, pas ni Bon Dieu . . .

BIASSOU

For the time being there is no God . . .

(BOUKMANN *turns to* BIASSOU.)

DESSALINES

Your magic could turn these dead into zombies.
An army of shadows that bullets would go through.
That would really frighten the French. Imagine.
A harvest of transparent soldiers. You have wounded.
You have dead. Save what you can. Come, start.
You need a good doctor. A white one.

(*He moves among the dead.* BOUKMANN, BIASSOU *help lift the wounded.*)

Scene 17

A camp. Night. TOUSSAINT *helping the wounded. He stops, exhausted.*

TOUSSAINT

. . . and now there has begun, after the revolt of Boukmann, such a series of savage, vicious scenes of hatred and revenge, such godless brutality, that I felt ashamed of my own race. For what they could not inflict on the army, they took out on the citizens. All the hatred and humiliation of a hundred years . . . You hear, Moise? (MOISE, *sitting quietly on a log, is watching his anguish.*) . . . of a hundred years is being accounted for. They sawed a planter in half between boards, they nailed a slave who tried to save his master, they nailed

him to a door. They are killing children, women . . . The
slave they nailed . . . I knew him. His name was Bartolo . . .

MOISE

They did us worse . . .

TOUSSAINT

We are supposed to be fighting a war.
To kill a child, that's a childish thing.

MOISE

Why don't you teach them?

TOUSSAINT

Teach them, at my age?
I put earth in their wounds, I soothe their orifices
With herbs, make poultices from country medicines,
And they cannot stop bleeding. The soil itself
Is bleeding, and I can't stop it. I don't want
Revenge, there's no strategy in revenge, Moise.

MOISE

You too good-hearted, Uncle. You want to see
The marks on my back?

TOUSSAINT

Bring me that hot water
And bring some clean rags. They're bringing
Their wounded. They're severely wounded

From murdering women, good niggers, and children,
And their good doctor Toussaint
Must look after them.

> (*He shouts.*)

NIGGERS!

> (*Silence.*)

NIGGERS! I AM HERE TO SERVE SOLDIERS, NOT
ANIMALS!

> (DESSALINES *enters the clearing with* BIASSOU *and*
> BOUKMANN. *They stop.*)

After you kill the women and children and the old planters,
after you burn the land and butcher the cattle and crucify
all the good niggers, THERE IS STILL THE ARMY!

> (DESSALINES *sits, chuckling. He restrains* BOUKMANN,
> *who moves, sword drawn, towards* TOUSSAINT. TOUSSAINT
> *sees him coming but ignores him, addressing the*
> GUERRILLAS.)

Now, all you great women killers and children killers and
good-nigger crucifiers have known me as Toussaint the
coachman, Toussaint the good doctor of this comical army
. . . Well, I did not leave to join a massacre. I came, at forty-
seven years old, to fight a war. I don't see any war. I see a
bunch of *crapons*, savages, I see nothing that is worth my
life. Well, it is very simple. There will now be an army, and
I will discipline that army. I'm old, but I've read the strategy
of war!

> (BOUKMANN *folds his arms and shakes his head.*)

Moise. Relieve General Boukmann of his sword.
The rest of you, get up on your feet,

Form fours, get your belongs together,
And prepare to march out of here.
> (*Silence.* MOISE *moves towards* BOUKMANN, *who keeps
> slicing the air around his head, and* MOISE *stops.*
> TOUSSAINT *goes over to* BOUKMANN.)

Look here, Boukmann. That is my nephew.
Now, don't waste my time. Come on, give me.

> (BOUKMANN *turns to* DESSALINES. DESSALINES *rises and
> moves among the* SOLDIERS.)

BOUKMANN

I don't need you all. I can fight alone.
I will start another army and you will see.
> (*He exits.*)

DESSALINES

Come on, come on, get off your black arses now, niggers,
All that foolishness is finished. You heard what the
Old man said. You going to be an army. You'll have
Nice uniforms, you coward goat fuckers, maybe even
    horses,
But right now you have to form fours and march. Come on.
> (*He moves among the* GUERRILLAS *kicking and slapping
> and drenching them with the hot water.*)

That is the way you want it, Uncle, right?
Attention!

Forward, march!

(*Desultorily, then more confidently, the* GUERRILLAS *march out of the grove.* TOUSSAINT *puts his arm around* DESSALINES. *They follow.*)

Scene 18

Exterior. Noon, Sunday. A patch of arable land behind YETTE*'s shack beyond the fields of Belle Maison. Church bells strike the noon Angelus.* POMPEY, *in a large straw hat, sweating, cursing as he ploughs.* YETTE *is in the shade of a single tree. She shouts, but he cannot hear.*

YETTE

Don't work so hard, is not your land,
And today is Sunday.
Come and drink something! Come!
(*She pours him some lemonade from a carafe.*)

POMPEY

Look at you. You stay in the sun so long
And you will get black.

YETTE

I glad. The white part of me is the town,
The black part of me is the country.
But the place coming well, and I thank you.

I thank you with all my heart, Pompey,
I don't think I was ever so happy.
Lie down, and I'll fan you with my hat.

(*She fans his body.*)

POMPEY

I must finish, I have to bring back the plough,
I have to . . .

YETTE

Lie down, Oh God.

Rest, *non?*

POMPEY

Somebody have to plant for people to eat.
Not everybody can be a soldier.
And they burning down this country . . .
All the estates . . . One day they could come here . . .

(YETTE *and* POMPEY *are in the shade. The wind cools
them, rustling the leaves* . . .)

YETTE

Is so nice here. I will never go back.
I can't believe that over on these hills
Niggers killing each other, people dying . . .
Is so quiet and happy here, I feel guilty.
And since you come on Sundays to help me with the land . . .
What I can tell you? . . .

POMPEY

Tell me you will never go. Say it again . . .

YETTE

You want all your women to be jealous . . .

POMPEY

Say it again. I finish with all of them . . .

YETTE

I am happy here. I am happy on this land.
I will never go anywhere again . . .

POMPEY

We will see . . .

YETTE

I swear on my cross.
(*She kisses her crucifix.*)
That poor mule in the sun . . .

POMPEY

You don't find the mule looking like Toussaint?
(POMPEY *juts out his lower lip,* YETTE *laughs. Silence.*
Peace.)
All Mr. Calixte do is sit around his room,
Praying that Monsieur Anton will come back . . .
But that old man Toussaint, victory after victory,
Battle after battle, and at his age.

(*He takes out a bamboo fife and begins to play.*)
Thank God for this peace.
And for you, too, my Yette.
Come in the house, I have something to show you.
(*He pulls her to him in the shade.*)

Scene 19

Exterior. Sunset. A long country road fenced with stakes.
TOUSSAINT, BIASSOU, DESSALINES, MOISE *walking. A*
severed head with a tricorn, with this sign nailed under it:

FRENCHMEN AND FREE-COLOUREDS

THIS NEGRO'S HEAD WAS BOUKMANN.

HERE IS THE FUTURE OF ALL

ENEMIES OF THE REPUBLIC.

DESSALINES

Read it, somebody! Biassou!

BIASSOU (*Reading.*)
Frenchmen and free coloureds,
This Negro's head was Boukmann.
Here is the future of all
Enemies of the Republic.

(DESSALINES *kisses the lips of the severed head, then hurls it*
away.)

DESSALINES

Adieu, Boukmann! Long live Dessalines.

Vive Jean Jacques Dessalines!

(*The troop moves on into the dusk.*)

Scene 20

Belle Maison. CALIXTE-BREDA *reading a letter.*

CALIXTE-BREDA

Pompey! Pompey! I heard from Monsieur Anton.

(POMPEY *runs in.*)

Listen. He has joined the mulatto army!

(*He reads.*)

If you love me, as you have always said, like your own son, then I ask you to help our cause against those who betrayed you, those who are now butchering those who have mixed blood, like your son, by sending us money to buy arms and ammunition to defend ourselves. After they have destroyed the whites, they will butcher the mulattos. Do not trust a single black. Toussaint, whom you treated like a younger brother, has shown you this. I am one of General Rigaud's trusted aides. This map will show you how to reach us. I do not expect to see you ever again, but if you should find it in your heart to see me again, you could be proud of me; I am, you see, Papa, no longer a weakling. I love you and forgive you because I have become

*a man, and it is as a man that I would like to face you
again.*

Come, Pompey, we will go to him. Come! Now!
> (*He paces the living room, pauses.*)

Pompey. You and I, we will find him.
You will help me find him, Pompey.
You know this country like your own hand.

> (*They exit.*)

Scene 21

Exterior. Day. A guerrilla camp in the mountains. A tent, a
SERGEANT *propped against a rock, eating. A shadow covers
him. He looks up, eating.* CHRISTOPHE.

SERGEANT

You are a major, I see.
> (*Pause.*)

What army?
> (CHRISTOPHE *turns away, bewildered. Then, back to the*
> SERGEANT.)

These days I can't tell one army from another.

CHRISTOPHE

Where is General Toussaint L'Ouverture?
> (*Exasperated, he explodes.*)

Attention! Salute.

(*The* SERGEANT *rises, spits.*)

SERGEANT (*Leisurely*)

. . . You in the wrong army, friend. You want Toussaint?
He gone to fight for the Spanish in San Domingo.

CHRISTOPHE

The Spanish?

SERGEANT

Dee Spaneesh. You know. Spaneesh. *Sí.*

CHRISTOPHE

                              Against his own country?

Why?

(*There is a howl of laughter.* DESSALINES *emerges from the
rear of the tent tying his trousers with a cord.*)

DESSALINES

Why? Ask Moise, his nephew. They went together.
Sonthonax offered him "the protection of the Republic"
If he will bring his army to his side.
                    (*He laughs.*)

CHRISTOPHE

Dessalines? You don't remember?
In the Place des Armes . . . years ago . . .

DESSALINES

The waiter. Yes. You're a soldier now.
A major.

CHRISTOPHE

I thought the time had come to fight together.

DESSALINES

You can read?

CHRISTOPHE

No.

DESSALINES

This sergeant can.
Listen to this from our esteemed commander.
Read. I admire that old bald-headed son of a bitch!

SERGEANT (*Reading.*)
The blacks want a king, and they will stop fighting
Only when that king is recognized.

DESSALINES

A king!
He is a royalist. All of this was for nothing.
(*He gestures.*)
He has printed another message for the armies.

CHRISTOPHE

A king?

SERGEANT (*Reading.*)
Brothers and friends. I am Toussaint L'Ouverture, my name is perhaps known to you. I have undertaken vengeance. I want liberty and equality to reign in San Domingo. I work to bring them into existence. Unite yourselves to us, brothers, and fight with us for the same cause . . .

(DESSALINES *looks out at the deserted camp.*)

DESSALINES

I turned to have a piss and they were gone.

Signed Toussaint L'Ouverture.

You know something?

We are going to join him.

(*He walks over to the* SERGEANT, *whose eyes are closed with exhaustion. He strips away his chevrons. The* SERGEANT *looks up, startled. A sword point slashes his cheek. He remains still.*)

This . . .

(*He holds up the chevrons.*)

Was when you served that coachman.

(*He throws it away.*)

That is when you serve me . . .

(*He points with his sword to the bleeding scar.*)

(*Fade-out.*)

Scene 22

Exterior. Day. Smoke. Noises far. A camp. Dark, overcast sky.
SOLDIERS, *some wounded, returning from battle.*
DESSALINES *emerges from a tent, an empty bottle in his*
hand, drunk.

DESSALINES

There must be one hundred thousand yellow niggers
slaughtered there.
Burn, burn! There's no more Les Cayes.
We have destroyed Rigaud!

(*Passes the bottle, hugs the* SERGEANT. *He dances a drunken*
dance, then stops, tottering as . . . CHRISTOPHE *arrives,*
muddy, tired. They watch the inferno.)

CHRISTOPHE

This is not war.

DESSALINES
It will do for now.
(TOUSSAINT *enters,* MOISE *with him.*)
Some rum?

TOUSSAINT (*Washing his hands.*)
I hate excess.

DESSALINES

Ho, ha! He kills ten thousand mulatto citizens
And shrugs his shoulders and says he hates excess!
I love this hypocrite!

(*He drunkenly embraces* TOUSSAINT.)

TOUSSAINT

Enough!

(*He paces angrily.*)

I come from an exhausting fight and find
My two best generals getting drunk like sergeants.
Collect your troops. We're marching out of here.
You too, General Moise.

(CHRISTOPHE, DESSALINES, MOISE *exit.*)

O God, to find in the centre of this whirlwind
Some core of quiet.

(*Enter two* SOLDIERS *with* CALIXTE-BREDA.)

SOLDIER

We found this one.

TOUSSAINT

Calixte? Monsieur Calixte? . . .

(*To the* SOLDIERS)

Leave us alone . . . Monsieur Calixte . . .

CALIXTE-BREDA

    And General Toussaint, not true?
I have walked for a week in the litter of your armies,
Passed through the fields burnt, rooted up
By army of wild pigs . . .

TOUSSAINT
  Pigs! My soldiers!

CALIXTE-BREDA
I stepped across dead children in the streets,
God in heaven, Toussaint. Hell is not worse.
(*He rushes to a table and seizes* TOUSSAINT'*s pistol. Hoists,*
     aims pistol.)
O God, give me the strength to shoot this monster.

TOUSSAINT
God. Do not speak of God, Monsieur Calixte.
I cannot think of God. Where was God in those years
When we were shipped and forced to bear our excrement,
Were peeled alive, pestered with cannibal ants,
Where was God?
(*He sits on a camp stool, weeping with rage and exhaustion.*)
I have learnt to pick up a dead child
On my sword as you would lift an insect.
I learnt this.
But when we tried, when we tried,
Where, where was your heart? Your God?

(CALIXTE-BREDA *is also weeping. The love between them*
pours out its bewilderment.)

CALIXTE-BREDA

Toussaint, what is all this,
What is happening to the world? To us?
When will there be peace?

TOUSSAINT

Do you know what peace means to me, monsieur?
It is a rag soaked in blood I must squeeze dry
Before there can be peace. And then
My generals say, Toussaint,
Leave him to clean it. Like your stables . . .

(*Enter* DESSALINES, CHRISTOPHE.)

DESSALINES

Who is this fucking white? A spy?

TOUSSAINT

I was his coachman.

DESSALINES

Coachman? Is he offering you your old job?
Look, this is not a fucking coachman, you white bitch,
This is General Toussaint L'Ouverture, commander in
    chief.
Kneel! On your knees! Kneel! Kiss his fucking foot!

CALIXTE-BREDA

So these are the great generals. Is this Dessalines?
And you. You are General Henri Christophe.

DESSALINES

Yes, yes, white man, this is Dessalines,
Who ripped the white heart from the flag of France.
Tell them you see him when you reach in hell.

TOUSSAINT

I command here, Jean Jacques.

(MOISE *enters.*)

MOISE

We ready to march.

CHRISTOPHE

Well?
(*To* TOUSSAINT)

Well?

TOUSSAINT

Look, you! Both of you, I will not be pushed! I will not.

DESSALINES

He hates excess.

CALIXTE-BREDA
Did you kill my son? Answer me that.

(*Silence.*)

TOUSSAINT
Take him, Sergeant.

SERGEANT
And . . .

DESSALINES
And shoot him, hang him, anything.
We have an army waiting for this ruin.

(*The* SERGEANT *waits.*
TOUSSAINT *in the tent. He is weeping.*
Outside, the army begins its march. The drums, the orders, the
chanting. The tent flap lets in light and the SERGEANT *enters.*
POMPEY, *manacled, is behind him, with another* SOLDIER.)

SERGEANT
General, you forget to tell us what to do with him.

(TOUSSAINT *looks up wearily.*)

TOUSSAINT
See that the body of the white is buried.
Let the priest say what he has to say over it.

SERGEANT

Yes, my General.

TOUSSAINT (*Rising with a groan.*)

It is yes, Comrade General.

It is always yes, comrade this and comrade that . . .

SERGEANT

Yes, Comrade General.

(TOUSSAINT *walks up to* POMPEY.)

TOUSSAINT

You saw what I did. You saw what I had to do?

(POMPEY *nods.*)

Are you afraid of me, too, Pompey?

(POMPEY *is silent.*)

You hid him, for all those years.

I suppose they would call you a good nigger.

You saw what I have had to do.

All that out there.

I myself, I thought war would be so . . . neat.

(*Pause.*)

I want to wage peace. To plant, where men fell.

Did we burn Belle Maison, too? Is it still there?

POMPEY

Oui, Comrade General . . .

TOUSSAINT

> And the stables, sweet dung,
And the great rooms intact?

POMPEY

It is good land.

TOUSSAINT

You loved it more than me, *compère*.

POMPEY

I would not say that, Comrade General.

TOUSSAINT

Where is Yette?
> (POMPEY *shakes his head, in tears.*)
You loved her, too, Monsieur Pompey.
And Belle Maison. It is yours now.
I'll write an order. We have to start . . . continue.
Wait. I will write an order giving you the estate.
You will manage it. You loved it the most.

POMPEY

I do not understand, Comrade General.
Mine? All that wide land? . . . Mine?

TOUSSAINT

It is yours. I will draw up the papers.
The land. Work it. Find Yette. And you both,
Together, slowly work it. You agree, don't you,
Jean Jacques?
> (*He embraces* DESSALINES.)

POMPEY (*Stepping near.*)
M'sieu Toussaint.

TOUSSAINT

Toussaint, Pompey. No. If you please.
Let him go, Sergeant. Give him a mule,
Food. Point the mule's head towards . . .
Anywhere . . . but away from here. This madness.
> (*He leads* POMPEY *away.*)

DESSALINES

Mais qui qualité moune i'croit moi y'est?

CHRISTOPHE

I don't know. What kind of person, Jacko?

DESSALINES

All this shit comes from speaking French like Frenchmen!
He "thou's" me. I'm not his subordinate
Or his familiar. His *tu* is too distant.
"*Et toi,* Jean Jacques," his arm around my shoulder,
Drawing me into his heart. I hate his heart,

I'd rip it from its cage and spit on it.
Do "thou" agree, waiter?

CHRISTOPHE

It's because thou can't read.

DESSALINES

I can read faces. That's all I need to read.

CHRISTOPHE

Read mine. Tell me what I will be after the war.
I can't read either. But I can see you, Jacko,
In a tight coat making speeches to Parliament.

DESSALINES

I don't want any more mouth-music about parliaments.
They just waiting till the war is finished, those
Ragtag and bobtail bunch of ragged blackbirds
In cravats and frock coats saying they're an Assembly,
Sitting on branches and calling themselves a Senate.
That's what you want? Me in a cravat and jacket
Making speeches that would make a statue sleep?
Senator Dessalines? Representative Dessalines?
I'd quicker go back to burning beef on a spit
And herding cows.

CHRISTOPHE

That was the revolution.
We fought it for the people, for the plebiscite.

DESSALINES

What words! What vocabulary! What nonsense!
Plebiscite! What is that? What is the language
To an idiot scratching his head in the country
And furrowing his forehead like a marmoset?
Words for parrots! We are tribesmen, *compère*,
Congolese, Arrabas, we have chiefs, we have kings,
No plebiscite! Mulatto words! Senate, plebiscite!
You think Boukmann would have said it? Smile!
If we surrender to this kind of language,
We surrender to their idea of civilisation,
And that way, in spite of victory, I tell you,
We would have won nothing. We will remain
One hundred, two hundred years from now, waiters,
Maids, servants, parrots, and monkeys. Plebiscite!
They will make mulattos of everybody.
Earth-coloured people who produce nothing.
I would slaughter every one of them again.

CHRISTOPHE

This was a military operation, Jacko,
That Toussaint ordered. And I follow orders.

DESSALINES

Come on, don't get your orders mixed up, waiter.
You used to serve them at the Auberge de la Couronne.
All of the trouble before the revolution

And all the problems after the revolution
Have come from this uncertain race, the mulattos,
From the impenetrable, rock-headed bourgeoisie,
Who, because they have hair like red wire, eyes
The colour of grey stones, would rather die
Than be called black. Well, since that's what they want,
Let them die, I'm giving them what they want.
They can go to heaven happy, and then us.
They won't see us anymore. We'll be in hell.

CHRISTOPHE
I don't know. I think we in hell already, mate.

(*They exit.*)

Scene 23

France. NAPOLEON *dictating. He screams at*
GENERAL LECLERC.

NAPOLEON
Who is this man? This gilded African? These are your
orders: "General Leclerc, follow your instructions exactly,
and the moment you have rid yourself of Toussaint,
Christophe, Dessalines, and the principal brigands, and
the masses of the blacks have been disarmed, send over
to the continent all the blacks and mulattos who have

played a role in the civil troubles . . . Rid us of these gilded Africans, and we shall have nothing more to wish."
Fini.

(*Pause. At the window.*)

Now we shall see who rules the New World!

ACT TWO

"Go, meet the angry kings . . ."

—Seneca

Scene 1

A BUGLER, *in French uniform, blows his sunset call, then leaves the battlement. The* CHORUS *enters. As she sings, to a slow drumbeat, sick* FRENCH SOLDIERS *are brought in on litters.*

CHORUS (*Singing.*)

Toutes c'est soldats français
Malades. Eux bien malades,
Ni ça ka prier Dieu
Ni ça qui ka rêver
C'est l'enfers eux rivées
La fièvre ka fait eux fous
Eux ka déchirer rades
Eux ka craser com' poux
Is sad, is very sad.

The army under Leclerc,
Their general, every day
Like flies they falling sick
With fever, yellow fever.
They tearing off their clothes.
The fever have them weak.
Some dreaming they in hell.
La guerre, c'est pas chose belle.

(*She exits to the drumbeat.*)

(*Saint-Domingue: Interior. Afternoon. An army hospital.*
LECLERC *in bed, sweating. He turns his head towards the*
mountains. PAULINE *enters, closes the door gently behind*
her. She is carrying a basin with cracked
ice, a napkin.)

LECLERC

I know how this bores you.
How you hate . . . sickness.
Like your brother, Napoleon.
Our short, great Emperor.
The corporal.
You have always done everything dutifully,
You measure the exact quantity of love, and no
More. I should be grateful. The Sister of my
Emperor.

PAULINE

You're tiring yourself.

        (*She mops his brow.*)

LECLERC

When you are weak, helpless like this,
You know what strength is.

PAULINE

    Sleep.

LECLERC (*Putting her hand away.*)

I'm afraid. Send in my secretary.

    (*Pause. The heat. The soft wind.*)

PAULINE

Don't be afraid, I love you. I wish you were well.

    (LECLERC *turns away, tears in his eyes.* PAULINE *looking*
      through the window at the afternoon mountains.)

I wish you were in France.
It would be simpler.

    (LECLERC *turns his head aside to sleep.* PAULINE *watches*
      him. Her face. She rises, takes up the basin. She goes to
      the window. She closes the window carefully. She exits
        behind a screen.)

Scene 2

Another part of the hospital. ANTON, *asleep.* PAULINE *enters the room. She agitates her loosened bodice gently and blows down the cleft of her bosom. She passes the damp cloth gently over her breast, then she shuts the door.*

LECLERC'S VOICE

... to the first consul, etc., etc., from Commander ... (*cough*) Commander in Chief, Army of Saint Domingue ... etc., etc. ... and the date ... what is the date?

ANOTHER VOICE

... bruary ninth ... eighteen nought two ...

LECLERC'S VOICE

... nought two ... I have great need of reinforcements. You must ... (*cough*) ... see how ... (*cough*) ... give me some water ... (*Images. The hospital. A* SOLDIER *in the gamboge dusk, looking out.*) I have already six hundred sick, the majority of my troops having embarked five months ago. Above all, count on my devotion ... I shall prove to France that you have made a good choice ... I need more men ... (*Images.* PAULINE *over the* SOLDIER. *Watching. He is gasping for breath.*) ... three months before our arrival ... Moise had sought to supplant Toussaint, and to do this, he had begun the massacre of six hundred to seven hundred white ... (*cough*) ... Toussaint had him shot and has rid us of him ... I have already more than one thousand, two hundred men in hospital, but I myself . . . (*cough*), am in excellent health . . . (*A* SURGEON *joins* PAULINE. *She goes to a window. The young* SOLDIER*'s face.*) . . . (*cough*) . . . the rainy season has arrived . . . Your sister remains as devoted and as true as ever to me, her hus . . . band (*cough*). Your devoted brother-in-law and general of the armies . . . You will have to sign for me . . . I cannot manage even a pen . . . Victor-Emmanuel.

SURGEON

Madame Leclerc, we must go.
We are moving this hospital.
The fever is worse here.
Anton Calixte just died.

(PAULINE *walking. She sees a black, half-naked* CHILD *and bends to it. She brings the* CHILD *to her caressingly. The army* SURGEON *emerges.* PAULINE *looks up. The* SURGEON *nods.* PAULINE *resumes playing quietly with the* CHILD.)

PAULINE

What is your name, eh? *Nom-ous? Ton nom?*

(*The* CHILD, *bewildered, doesn't answer. The bugle blowing. Fade-out.*)

Scene 3

An army camp. DESSALINES, CHRISTOPHE. THREE
PRISONERS, *stripped, are waiting.* TOUSSAINT *crosses to the*
PRISONERS. *He looks them over rapidly, his face a cold fury,*
then taps one on the chest.

TOUSSAINT

You remember my orders?
Ous save ça ous fait?
Ous songer mes ordres?
You know what you did?

     (PRISONER *spits.* TOUSSAINT *turns to him.*)
It amuses me. Tell my why you spat, comrade?

PRISONER (*Spitting.*)

You would not know me.
I'm a nigger. I fought the French with you.
Now look at this. Look at you.
You are a busy man, General.

(TOUSSAINT *looks him up and down.*)

TOUSSAINT

Pity. You are a good Haitian.
Bad soldier. You had your orders.
And this spitting business. *Pas bon.*
Continue! Shoot them!

(*The* PRISONERS *are taken away. Orders ring out. The* PRISONERS *are shot.*)

. . . and we made this agreement with the French; I have made it, if you want, for the good of this new country, but that, not even that, is the business of this army. You disobeyed orders, you fought these dragoons when I ordered a cease-fire. Those men behind me there, those French dragoons, are our brother soldiers now, because I, yes I, *moi*, Toussaint, made this agreement with General Leclerc . . . (MOISE, *in full dress but bareheaded, in the evening drizzle, in front of the brigade.*) But General Moise decided that he would disobey. Who here does not know that Moise is my own nephew? But I do not love him more than I love this country . . . I have nothing to ask Moise. But I have something to ask of you. You will show these French dragoons what Haitian soldiers are . . . (*Silence.*) You will step forward, all of you, to a man, with your guns loaded, reversed, and you will shoot yourselves. Reverse arms! One step forward, march! Prepare to fire! (*The ranks of* SOLDIERS *have stepped past* MOISE. TOUSSAINT *'s voice, hoarsely.*) Fire! (*The* SOLDIERS *fall. Silence.* MOISE *steps forward, looks* TOUSSAINT *in the eyes, removes his pistol.*)

MOISE

I can shoot myself.

(*He shoots himself.*)

TOUSSAINT

Forward, march!

(*The army moves on.*)

(*Fade-out.*)

Scene 4

Exterior. Night. Le Cap: partially ruined buildings. POMPEY *hitches his mule in the street, outside the decaying façade of a pension. He looks towards the windows. A half-naked* WHORE *screams at him and slams the jalousies.*

WHORE

Maquereau!

(*Laughter within.* POMPEY *enters the salon. Dancing.* SOLDIERS, *some white,* WHORES. POMPEY *inquires. He climbs a stair cautiously, knocks at a door. A* FRENCH GRENADIER *opens it. He is finishing dressing.*)

GRENADIER

Take your time, citizen.
   (*Over his shoulder to* YETTE *in the bed beyond him.*)
I didn't know you took niggers, too, empress.

(*He salutes* POMPEY, *exits.* YETTE *lies in bed. Jaded.*
Smoking. Silence. She turns her head away.)

POMPEY

Reviens, chérie, reviens. I beg you.
It have nothing here for you, Yette.
I don't care how they mash you up.
I know it is the war. I know it is all these people.
Listen, they do not know you like I know you.

(YETTE*'s face. She rises, sits up on the bed.*)

YETTE

I'm no good for you. This is where I belong.

POMPEY

You know how long I looking for you, Yette? Three months.
And listen. The government, they give me in charge, me . . .
Me. This big house. They make me responsible,
Me, stupid Pompey that you use to laugh at "little boy."
Are you not tired, eh, Yette, my Yette? Don't this life make
You old? So come with me. You want me on my knees inside
    this place?
I will kneel down. You want me to make jokes?
I will make jokes. The land is a hard mother, but it can
Make more children.
        (YETTE *lies back in bed, her face in the pillows.*)
            Well, laugh, *non?*

YETTE

I leave you. Why you want me for?
A whore is all I can do. I hate the earth.
I hate the Haitian earth. Why? Tell me.

POMPEY

Why I want you? Because I want to see you with your arms
brown and shining picking the corn that will die if you do
not come. I want to hear you laughing like the water when
you washing the two clothes we have. Because it is the time
of peace. The war will finish. The white soldiers who have
money, they will go home. Then where you will go? It will
have no more soldiers. I will walk by the mule I have
outside one thousand hundred miles, and we will reach to
the old house. And the high bed there, Yette, and the wind
that coming from the mountains where you belong, so say
yes, Yette. Or don't say yes, just even shake your head, a little
so, and we will go. Now. Or in a little while. But you and I,
we is Haiti, Yette.

YETTE (*In tears, nodding.*)

I have a few little things I have to get. But yes.
Yes, *Ti-moune*. I will come.

POMPEY

Our house. *Merci, Bon Dieu.*

(YETTE *dresses. They exit into the streets.*)

Scene 5

GENERAL LECLERC *at the window.*

LECLERC

After he's dead let them fight over him,
Christophe the waiter, Dessalines the madman,
Those two black buzzards circling his carcass.

Scene 6

A camp. Shacks. SOLDIERS.
Interior. Night. A tent.

DESSALINES (*Shouting.*)

We did what we had to do. That is all!
C'est tout, Henri. Fini! I want to hear nothing.
We sold him to the Frenchmen. I don't want to hear.

CHRISTOPHE

Well, you goddamn will hear!

DESSALINES

Qui qualité jurer ça?

Goddamn. You will goddamn well hear! *Gadez*,
Me. *Nègre.* African. Not Eeenglesh. *Comprend?*
I don't got to goddamn well hear nothing, gentlemen.
I got to goddamn eat.

(CHRISTOPHE *lunges, turns him around.* DESSALINES
pauses, disentangles himself.)

You cannot be serious.

CHRISTOPHE

To feel it. That is all.

To feel it. What we did him. You and me!
Remorse! Jean Jacques.

DESSALINES

Remorse . . . *bien.* All right.

Why did you sell him to Leclerc?

CHRISTOPHE (*Hoarsely, wearily*)

For peace. I sold him, as you put it, monsieur,
So that at least this country could have peace,
Because my hand is weak from massacre,
Because I cannot remember the last time I have seen
An ordinary man, a man without a wound.
Give him some honour.

DESSALINES

Honour?

CHRISTOPHE

Yes!

DESSALINES

Do you remember when he turned on that same nigger that gave him his command "The Brigadier" Biassou? That was after he joined the Spanish. You remember Moise? And how he loved Calixte? That was when he was for a king. We went with him, right? And then he turned against the Spanish, and we turn with him? So what is all this shit about dishonour?

CHRISTOPHE

Talk quietly. The officers will hear.

DESSALINES

I will speak quietly, *compère*, and now let me tell you what I remember: I remember Moise, his own nephew that he commanded to execute himself. I remember that smart little monkey of a coachman betraying his own country, *his own country*, to the Spanish, without a reason, none. I remember when you came up to his camp and he had packed his bag of monkey tricks and jumped over the border, to come back fighting his own people, for another set of whites, and if you and me had asked him, he would have said what you said: "I did it for the sake of peace." So I do not give a particular fuck what the French do with him, whether Bonaparte puts him in a cage in his public gardens for little blond French children to throw bananas at. (*Pause. The two watch each other.*)

Look, we have done it, we have a whole country to rule

now, we begin again by betraying the French, after this! We divide it according to the campaigns. You are a general. Let us go back to work. Have a bad night. Have bad dreams if you want, but tomorrow: work.

(*They exit.*)

Scene 7

Aboard ship. A cabin. Dusk. TOUSSAINT, LECLERC, *others.*

LECLERC

This letter is from my Emperor, who is now yours also.

(*He reads.*)

As regards the return of the blacks to the old regime, the bloody struggle out of which you have just come victorious with glory commands us to use the utmost caution . . . For some time yet vigilance, order, a discipline at once rural and military, must take the place of the positive and pronounced slavery of the coloured people of your colony. Especially the master's good usage must reattach them to his rule. When they shall have felt by comparison the difference between a usurping and tyrannical yoke—And I think he means yours, Excellency—*And that of the legitimate proprietor interested in their preservation*—By which he means himself of course—*then the moment will have arrived for making them return to their original condition*—Naturally he means

slavery—*from which it was so disastrous to draw them.* So
then are my orders clear?

TOUSSAINT

General Leclerc, I was a slave. I understand.

LECLERC

Oh, we must clarify the distinction, General.
You are not our slave exactly but our prisoner.
A hostage to peace. A contract arranged
Between France and your comrade generals.
You may hoist sail, Captain.

(*The* CAPTAIN *looks in.*)

CAPTAIN
Excellency . . .
(*He exits.*)

TOUSSAINT

How far do I go, monsieur?

LECLERC

Quite far.

TOUSSAINT

For . . . for how long?

(LECLERC. *Silence. Then . . .*)

LECLERC

I don't manage these things. That's up
To the First Consul.

TOUSSAINT

I have served France.

LECLERC (*Wryly*)

You have served everybody.

TOUSSAINT (*At the window.*)

I served her.
That place.

LECLERC

Why do we call countries women?
We see them as wives or whores. It is a piece of earth.
Frankly, I was hoping to avoid all of this sentiment.
I was hoping that you would not have forced me
To harden my heart. I admire your genius.
So do your two generals, Dessalines and Christophe.

TOUSSAINT

They betrayed me to my enemy so that there could be
    peace?

They aren't Africans but slaves. Pets of your empire. Swine,
    not panthers!

LECLERC

Besides, I'm not sure that what protects you from tribal
    genocide
Isn't this very empire that you mock. Before it, you were
    hungry
Wolves drinking the wind, tearing one another with your
    teeth.

TOUSSAINT

We have no wolves here. Wild boars, yes. Illiterate. Both of
them.

LECLERC

Whichever predator you prefer. But with it, not only a
common hate herded you together, but I'm tired of
metaphor, I'm a rational man, a soldier with fever, not
delirium, before it, wolves, boars; but with it, under it,
under the French flag with its three colours, its three
principles, you straightened up from animals to men. It is
discipline that straightened your spine. It is our laws,
our books, our courts, our language, our uniforms, our
architecture that you would like to practise now, isn't that
correct? Then why be wolfish, why bite the hand that fed
you? That taught you to add and write?

TOUSSAINT

I have always appreciated that. But those are ideals, as much as the Christian Church is an ideal. The empire wasn't built on that, General.

LECLERC

I am talking about civilisation!

TOUSSAINT

I am remembering civilisation. All those glorious white marbles in your museums, all your Gothic arches, your embroidered books. What do they mean to a slave whose back is flayed so raw that, like a book, you can read the spine? I should be talking to your cousin-in-law the Emperor. We are not equals in rank. I wouldn't discuss civilisation with my corporals.

LECLERC

Come, Commander General, you are more than that.

(*A sail is hoisted, creaking.*)

TOUSSAINT

       I am not the Commander General.
My name is François-Dominique Toussaint,
I am a coachman. I was employed under the kind care
Of Monsieur Calixte-Breda. I also suffer from . . .
   hallucinations,

Brought on by old age and the toothache,
And I have had, Doctor, this persistent dream
That all slaves, brothers, Africans, whatever,
Would follow me, this coachman, towards . . . towards . . .
    towards . . .
They have hoisted the sail. The longboat is ready.
You must go. The earth is cracked. There is division among
The soldiers. There must be peace.

                        LECLERC

Call yourself a hostage to peace, General.
And you promise the First Consul to cooperate
For the sake of peace; that when you are in exile
You will not try to make use of your authority?

                        TOUSSAINT

                                        My authority?

When this voice had authority it lived
In expectation of an echo. By the sea, armies!
Breakers throwing their caps in the air!
Lances of men bowed to it like the canes.
Now it's an old man's cough. Rattling gravel
In a riverbed. My tongue is a dry leaf. The sun has set
In my throat. My authority is hoarse. A child
Wouldn't obey it. Much less hear it. No, sir,
You needn't worry about my authority.
Any more than Moise.

LECLERC

You mean Moise, your general?
Isn't he dead?

TOUSSAINT

He lives in his uncle.
When his uncle dies, General Moise will die.
But they will die with me, every one of them
Who believed I saved this country for myself.
In those days when I had authority.

LECLERC

Don't smile at me as if I laid a trap.
It was your own generals who approached me.

TOUSSAINT

The thought is common, the execution expected.
Nothing should startle a government, treaties, betrayals,
And done out of expediency, not friendship.
Once, I changed sides myself, and it surprised them.
I often wonder why I fought this war.
The war had all it needed, in campaigning.
For strategy: Christophe, for fury: Dessalines.
Why was I there? To curry-comb their horses?
Now they have offered me a greater choice than war
Without even my asking them. What a gift;
What, ultimately, an exact compensation.
To make myself a sacrifice, if not for war,

But for the original intention: peace.
I'll go to my exile as Moise went to his,
That one where there is no passport needed,
No shadowy customs. He will say "Uncle,"
I'll embrace him.

LECLERC
I know. General . . .
(*He extends his hand.*)
Adieu.

TOUSSAINT (*Taking it.*)
We have been good enemies. Perhaps the First Consul
Will treat me as you have.

(LECLERC *descends the ship's side.*)

LECLERC
Oh, I'm sure of that. Now,
After this, you will be confined to your cabin.
Take a long, last look at those mountains, General.

TOUSSAINT
Haiti, adieu.

(LECLERC *climbs onto the pier. The ship moves out of the
harbour. Music. Fade-out.*)

Scene 8

Belle Maison. Interior. Night. The quarters. YETTE *goes
to the earthen oven and prepares supper. Her back turned
to* POMPEY, *entering. He embraces her, wearily, from
habit.*

POMPEY

Ça raide. Is hard. All the men going.
They tired of the earth. The last one, Félix,
Leave today, to join the army.

YETTE

Which one?

POMPEY

You know Félix.
How you mean "which one"?
He always watching you.

YETTE

Which army?
(*She comes to the crude table with the pot.*)

POMPEY

How I know which army? It have so many.
Maybe Christophe, maybe Dessalines, maybe
Pétion, maybe even Leclerc. Or with your
People, the mulattos, Royer and Pétion.

YETTE

My people. So is my people again?

POMPEY (*Touching her hand.*)

Pardon, but I tired. The mule is sick.

(*He begins eating.*)

They say that Dessalines, and some say even
Christophe, hunting down our people, all the
Blacks, under the orders of General Leclerc.

YETTE

You must wear that nasty cloth?
If you want a serviette when you eating, tell me
And I will wash one. But I can't bear to see it.
I hate when you wipe your mouth on your sleeve.

(POMPEY, *hurt, stops eating. His eyes flicker with the old
fear of her restlessness.*)

POMPEY

All right. You see me, *hein*? Making pose.
I thought you would like it. For manners.
You know, like the aristocrats.

(*A silence. Night outside. The insects, and the wind.*)

You not going to eat, then?

(YETTE *moves away to the oven. She pauses there, her
back to him.*)

Yette?

Qui ça?

(Silence. The night. The wind.)

Tell me.

I can take it.

YETTE

Yes. You so strong. So nice. So good.

Is I who am nothing.

No. Don't come by me.

(POMPEY *sits back down. He looks into his bowl. He swallows*
dryly, his head down.)

I want the strength.

(She turns.)

Ti-moune . . .

(She turns away again.)

All this, all this, is only sadness for me, Pompey.

Since I was a girl I know this war. Here is,

Well, different. Is pretty, true. Is really, really pretty . . .

(POMPEY *silently, expressionlessly, weeping.)*

I know you crying, but I must still talk. I see you in the field
there, you alone, planting, you and the damn mule, and I
know how much you love the earth. And I wish I could love
you like you love the earth. But in the war, when I was with
the soldiers, even the white soldiers, even when I used to
feel so shame, I know I was not for this country life. Maybe
because I have their blood in me. French blood. Maybe I
want all that. My life is Le Cap. But sometimes I does
just feel, at my age, like an old black woman up in the
mountains with my teeth going, my body getting dry, and

nothing to do but cook white yam and a piece of saltfish for
you. You understand what I am saying? . . .

(YETTE *turns to* POMPEY. *He has turned sideways in his
chair, to avoid her pity.*)

POMPEY

I understand. You asking to go.
You are too fine for all of this. Is true.

YETTE

I suppose so. I don't know. To go again.
I didn't know I could say it.

POMPEY

They say there is nothing in Le Cap now,
Since General Christophe burn it. But
There is what you want. Not that?

YETTE

Look, I am weak?

POMPEY

What you asking me, woman?

YETTE

If I am weak?

POMPEY

Ask yourself that. Ask God that. Not me.
You cannot expect me to say that.

YETTE

They give you this big house
And you will not live in it. Look at us.
Look at it. Up there, empty. Look how we live,
Eat. It is yours. You frightened to go in it.
You bring me back here. To live how I used to.
Look at your clothes. There are clothes in that house.

POMPEY

What you doing to me, woman?
What kind of man you making out of me?

YETTE

Don't beg me, then, *Ti-moune*. Tell me.
Give me an order like a soldier. Tell me to go!
You was never a soldier. Try. Like a soldier to his whore.
Order me stay and I will stay. Otherwise, otherwise,
Oh God, what will happen to me?
          (*She is at his knees, sobbing.*)

POMPEY

Stay.

          (*Pause.*)

Stay. Not for me. But because
There is nothing else. Now let me eat.

And from now on, we will live.

    (YETTE *rises, wipes her face. She shakes her head.*)

We will live the way you want to. Clothes, lace.

Servants, if you want servants. You deserve it.

YETTE

It was not for that . . .

POMPEY

Maybe. But that is where we will live, anyway.

Over there. When I finish in the earth,

I will come into the big house, a different

Man. Not to please you. But it will be Pompey, *le*

    Bourgeois;

Pompey, the man of property. It will be amusing, for

A while. Here. Money. Go into Le Cap and buy some

    clothes.

YETTE

That is not what I want, *Ti-moune.*

        (*She sits opposite him.*)

I was just tired.

POMPEY

Nevertheless, we will do that.

YETTE

Moi aimais-ou Ti-moune.

I love you for yourself, Pompey.

POMPEY

Yes.

(*He resumes eating.*)

As usual, this is good.

(Y E T T E *watches him, and shakes her head slowly with a
pitying admiration. Fade-out.*)

Scene 9

France. Interior. A room in Napoleon's palace. N A P O L E O N
seated before a fireplace and an A I D E.

A I D E

Are you too tired, Excellency?

N A P O L E O N

Read the next one. And after that, enough.
Who is it from?

A I D E (*Reading.*)

Toussaint L'Ouverture. From the prison in the Jura Mountains.

N A P O L E O N

I know where it is. I put him there.

A I D E (*Reading.*)

*I have had the misfortune to incur your anger; but as to
fidelity and probity, I am strong in my conscience, and I have*

to say with truth that among all the servants of the State none is more honest than I. I was one of your soldiers and the first servant of the Republic in San Domingo. I am today wretched, ruined, dishonoured, a victim of my own services. Let your sensibility be touched at my position . . . (Interior. Snow falling. A cell in the Jura Mountains. A TURNKEY *enters a cell. He goes to* TOUSSAINT, *starved, hollow, shrunken, asleep, and shakes him. The body does not move.)*

. . . Be touched at my position, you are too great in feeling and too just not to pronounce on my destiny . . . Signed Toussaint L'Ouverture . . .

There is a doctor here. He wants to see you.

(*The* DOCTOR *enters.*)

DOCTOR

I had to examine the body to confirm it.
He looked as shrivelled as a marmoset.
                    (*He goes to a window.*)
All the snows of the Jura didn't whiten him.
His hair was the grey of soiled snow. Blizzards
Whiten out memory, pines disappear,
And men walking through clouds
Are faint as angels. When I found him
He was as black and cold as the bars
Of his cell. He was coiled like a child.
They might have given him an extra blanket.
It's snowing hard there now. It's the season,
But there's no blizzard that can obliterate him.

The wind keeps scattering those torn-up treaties
We made with him, all in the name of peace.
There's no peace deeper than a winter peace.
A cold, white peace. They'll bury him up there.
In Haiti, two jackals fight for his carcass.
The autopsy is there, a white report
With its black characters. Am I dismissed?

NAPOLEON

Yes.

(*The* DOCTOR *exits.*)

Are there any more letters?

(*Fade-out.*)

Scene 10

Haiti. Exterior. POMPEY *in the field, with
a few other* WORKERS.

POMPEY

This earth getting too dry.
We need some rain.

(*A conch shell. Then bells. A* PEASANT, *shouting from far off,
runs onto the field.*)

PEASANT

We have a king, Monsieur Pompey! You hear the bells?
Long live the Emperor Jean Jacques the First.

POMPEY

Stop this foolishness.
Why Dessalines must be King?

PEASANT

Because Toussaint is dead.
They hold him.

YETTE

Bon Dieu. Bon Dieu.
Haïti fini. Haiti is finished.
Haiti is finished. Look, the sun dark.

PEASANT

All you didn't know? Pompey, Monsieur Pompey?

POMPEY

Where is the rain now? Where is Moise?
You remember the night of the cane fires we was dancing?
Then the rain fall and we went inside and shelter?
Where is Biassou, the one-handed general? And
Where are the days that the earth smell of rain,
And the horses that bowed their necks to his hand?
Where is all that? From now on,

Water will taste different. Grass smell different.
And this, the Haitian earth, different.
We cannot do no more work today. Go home.
Fold up your hopes to show them to your children.
Because after him, now come
The angry kings.
God help us men.

Scene 11

Cap Haitien, 1805. Interior, the cathedral. The altar.
ARCHBISHOP BRELLE *kneeling. A* CHOIR. *Behind*
BRELLE, *as he bows, the also kneeling figure of*
DESSALINES. *Dimly, farther, in the dark pews, below the*
soaring arches, in full regalia, the GENERALS,
CHRISTOPHE. BRELLE *reaches for the jewel-encrusted*
crown. The music soars, he moves solemnly towards
DESSALINES. *From the squares and the military*
emplacements outside the cathedral, cannon thunder.
DESSALINES, *crowned, with sceptre, acknowledging homage*
from the GENERALS. *He accepts the homage, more fear in its*
extravagance of gesture than homage, and abruptly, but
grinning, indicates . . .

DESSALINES
Assez. C'est bien assez, merci.
Merci, merci, merci . . .

(DESSALINES *indicates that he would like to move on. The emperor moves, the entourage begins to move. Near the emperor is another black* GENERAL.)

GENERAL

And now that we have a black emperor, Your Majesty,
We expect, of course, a black nobility.

(DESSALINES *stops. The entourage stops.*)

DESSALINES

A black nobility? *Moi seul, je suis noble!*
I alone am noble! Christophe! I appoint you . . .
    (*Then he progresses, laughing. The entourage progresses.*)
Secretary of Agriculture. You will prepare
A tour of my kingdom. The states, the houses . . .
We have to make our people go back to the earth!
Now tell the wild boar that I killed on the beach,
When my arse was exposed to the wind, go on;
Find his carcass where the flies sang their hymns
And tell him you saw me. The Emperor Dessalines.
That I alone am noble! Remember that! *Moi seul!*
    (*He exits, acknowledging cheers, mounts to the balcony, others following.*)

Scene 12

Interior. Night. The ballroom at Belle Maison. Hundreds of candles, banners. Liveried ATTENDANTS. MUSICIANS *in an alcove on a level overlooking the ballroom floor. A flag, with a portrait of the Emperor Jean Jacques Dessalines. Trumpets, applause.* DESSALINES *enters with his* GENERALS, BRELLE, *and court.* YETTE, POMPEY *waiting on the stairs.*

DESSALINES

So. This is the house where Toussaint was a coachman. Did you know that, Henri? This is the house. Well, we will show you tonight! You hear me, house? Tonight! I'll make your old arse rattle! (POMPEY *and* YETTE *descend the stairs.*) Our host, Citizen Pompey! I present my wife, the Empress; my daughter, Celimène, coming behind her; Monseigneur Corneille Brelle—as you see, citizen, we still respect the Church. The bishop crown me Emperor seven weeks before Bonaparte was crowned at Notre Dame. My Minister of Agriculture, Citizen General Henri Christophe, his secretary Baron Citizen Pompey, Valentin Vastey. Vastey. You see. Look at this council, every colour is here, and these are?

POMPEY

My wife . . . Yette . . .

(DESSALINES *lasciviously holds on to her hand.*)

DESSALINES

Enchanté. Ravissante. We dance: I have brought my musicians.
Eux aimaient toute ça, bien, eh, Christophe?
I say, they like all this, eh?
A little colour. This black majesty!
What music should I dance to, Archbishop?
I will show your grace my grace! Ha! What?

BRELLE

You know, when it's harvest time for the canes,
Your people have a mock war. They split in factions,
This one adores the rose, this one the daisy
They call La Marguerite. With wooden swords, with
    feathers
Plucked from the canes in arrow, they sing
These tender battle hymns; they march, they die.
I wish this war was what they did, that our corpses
Were slain for flowers. What a perfume
Would saturate the Haitian earth instead.
To faint from sweetness at the smell of peace.

(*A* La Comette *dance. The* DANCERS *waltz and freeze, waltz
    and freeze.* VASTEY *and* CHRISTOPHE *watching*
    DESSALINES *and* YETTE *dancing.* POMPEY *leans
    against a wall.*)

CHRISTOPHE

Call him Jacques the jacko, jackass, anything but an
    emperor!

What kind of emperor is this, Vastey? Listen, you see how
he

Divides the estates among his ex-soldiers? By his nose.
This

Is a government by that nigger's nostrils, his mud-foot
veterans

Bring him scraps of paper deeds, forgeries, they are the
deeds

With smoke, and this medalled jackass who cannot read
sniffs

And then pronounces on their merit. A nose rules us,
friend.

A nose is my Emperor. I make policy. I must look after
his

Agriculture, and he does that!

He wants Haiti to be black, so he does this by bleeding it
white.

VASTEY

The revolution made him what he is, General.

CHRISTOPHE

Don't call me general. I am in agriculture.

But I have learnt one thing from it.

(*Pause.*)

That pig should be butchered.

Tell him I'm tired and I've gone to bed.

(*He exits, climbing the stairs.*)

Scene 13

Interior. The MUSICIANS *weary, playing. Hours later. Other guests asleep. The royal family absent.* DESSALINES *and* YETTE *still dancing.* DESSALINES *barefooted.* POMPEY *stirs, wants to move towards* DESSALINES. DESSALINES *notices. He stops dancing. The music stops. He strides, totters over to* POMPEY.

DESSALINES

You want to sleep, citizen?

Go to bed. Your Emperor's permission.

Go to bed. The cock is crowing.

Go!

   (*He pushes him out.* POMPEY *moves.* YETTE *stands alone, sweaty, dishevelled.*)

Your wife will be all right.

Your Emperor's assurance.

     (*To* YETTE)

You will be all right, yes?

     (YETTE *nods wearily. To* POMPEY)

Music! Music! You are not married, not true?

     (POMPEY *shakes his head no.* DESSALINES *claps his hands.*)

Then tomorrow, first thing, I will marry you.

Not me! But the archbishop! A white archbishop!

     (*He returns to* YETTE, *dances.*)

A real archbishop, citizen. And white.

And a real emperor. Now go to sleep.
You will need all your little strength tomorrow night.
(POMPEY withdraws. To YETTE)
And tonight, my honey-colour negresse,
Tonight you and I will make a prince,
A little present for your husband.
Maybe twins. What is wrong?
I understand. You are tired.
Come. Come with me. *Assez?*
(*The music stops. He claps his hands, indicating they should*
all leave. The remnants of guests who still have the strength
go off. Some cross the fields, meeting the dawn.)
Come to the balcony to see your kingdom.
Smell the air. Morning.
Morning in Haiti. What is your
Name again, mulatresse?

YETTE

Yette, Your Majesty.

DESSALINES

Come to the balcony to smell the morning, Yette.
(They move out to the balcony.)
Your Majesty.
(Laughs.)
Suppose . . .
Suppose I let you call me Jacques?
(*The balcony. Morning. Fresh. Stirring.* YETTE *exhausted*
but lovely. The cool wind.)

I mean to say what is that for us, Your Majesty!
You making love and jumping under me, crying
Uh—uh!—uh, Your Majesty. And afterwards,
Thank you, Your Majesty. It is ridiculous, not true?

(YETTE *says nothing.*)

A lovely day. The morning. Fresh. The breeze.
Like a cool tongue on a woman's thigh.

YETTE

Let me go, sir.

DESSALINES

Rub your arm on these muscles. Feel.
. You feel how smooth and black they are, mulatresse?
Do you like an emperor made of pure ebony?
This is your own flesh, your grandfather's flesh.
And look into my eyes now and find your pride.
Like the skin of a trotting panther, yes, black
Like the galloping panther that carries
Two yellow candles in his eyes, whose pads
Are quiet as ashes, whose teeth are fine bone,
Who has the night for his cave, whose skin
Smells of the jungle, and whose eyes are stars
Searching the heaven for a face like yours.
I'm like a black candle melting when you touch me.

YETTE

S'ous plait.

DESSALINES

Do not beg me.

I cannot stand people to beg me.

(*Pause.*)

Look, that is not your husband in the grass there?

Sitting out in the dew. Crying into the dew,

A big man like that? You married a child!

YETTE

No. He is a man. As much as you.

DESSALINES

I thought I tell him to go somewhere else.

He disobey his Emperor. Well, maybe

He does not want his room.

You have heard what I do men who disobey me?

YETTE

Yes. Don't hurt him.

DESSALINES

Hurt him? Me?

Listen, you will not believe it,

But you will boast when you are an old woman

How, in that same room, you fucked a king.

(*He waves to* POMPEY, *makes a sign on his lips of silence,
and moves from the balcony with* YETTE.)

Scene 14

Interior. Dark. The bedroom. Dawn. DESSALINES, YETTE *in bed. Half-dark.* DESSALINES *on* YETTE.

DESSALINES

... *dit* ... *Jacques* ... Call me Jack.

YETTE (*Softly*)

... Your Majesty ... Your Majesty.

DESSALINES

... *Jacques* ... *dit Jean Jacques* ...

YETTE (*Her eyes open, dry.*)

... Your ... Majesty ... Majesty ...

DESSALINES (*Slapping her.*)

... *Jacques* ... *salope! Jacques!*

YETTE (*Wincing; tears begin.*)

... Majesty ... Majesty ...

DESSALINES (*Slapping her.*)

... Say it ... Yellow bitch ... you sweet
Yellow bitch ...

(*He slaps her.*)

... say Jacques! Jacques! Jacques!

YETTE (*Quietly*)

... *Nègre* ... *nègre* ... *cochon!*

(DESSALINES *slaps her frenziedly to a climax.*)

DESSALINES

That's better. Better. Yes ... *Nègre* ...
          (*He rolls off. Watching the ceiling.*)
Yes ... *c'est ça moi y est* ...
              (*Pause.*)
Un nègre ...
            (*He turns to her.*)
Merci. I thank you.
          (*He removes a ring.*)
Here. Take it. For your wedding.

(*Fade-out.*)

Scene 15

Dawn. The same, but the yard. DESSALINES *enters the yard
and shouts towards the arches of the Great House.*

DESSALINES

It's sunrise. Wake up. Where is my Minister
Of Agriculture? Christophe! Minister Christophe.
         (*He crows like a cock.*)
The cock is trumpeting, Minister of Agriculture.
And the golden cock, your Emperor, is calling you.

(CHRISTOPHE, *partially dressed, comes out onto the
balcony, then descends.* DESSALINES *is in a corner
of the yard, peeing.*)

Peace. I hate peace. I piss on peace.

(CHRISTOPHE *joins* DESSALINES.)

Pee with me, Minister. That is a command.

CHRISTOPHE

You should get some sleep, Jean Jacques.

DESSALINES

Pétion and his mulatto army are over there
Behind those blue hills. He will not fight me.
He hides in the south. Look at these hills,
This earth, how dry it is. I sprinkled it.
I sprinkled it with an emperor's golden dew.
Kings will grow out of this soil; my seed
Will grow more emperors.

CHRISTOPHE

Kings. Yes.

And the peasants cut them down.

DESSALINES

I must lend you my crown sometime, Henri.

CHRISTOPHE

Make it a crown of olive, Your Majesty.

DESSALINES

Olive? What is it?

CHRISTOPHE

A tree. The crown of peace.

DESSALINES

Ah yes. Peace. You know when peace will be?
When every yellow skin in Haiti goes dry as corn.
When we bury all the treacherous mulattos.
We had dusty times in those hills, though, General.
Boukmann. I kissed his head. Remember that?
Now it is time for me to administer justice.
These people will not plant.
They must go back to planting.
You hear me, Minister of Agriculture?
Now bring in the one who refused to work.

CHRISTOPHE

No more whipping. They have been beaten enough.
I have to protect them, to encourage them.
You need sleep.

DESSALINES

Bring him in front me.
The one who wouldn't plant.

CHRISTOPHE

No more whipping.

DESSALINES

No more whipping? Don't we whip mules, horses?
When they don't move? What's wrong?
What are you staring at, Minister of Agriculture?

CHRISTOPHE

An animal.

DESSALINES (*Turning.*)
What animal? Where?

CHRISTOPHE

You can't see him.

DESSALINES

Why? A ghost?

CHRISTOPHE

You would have to be where I am to see him.

DESSALINES

M'as comprends. Stand where you are to see an animal?
I am standing next to you and I cannot see him.

CHRISTOPHE

I can smell him.

DESSALINES

Yes? What smell? Close?

CHRISTOPHE

Very close. He is here, a spine-backed boar,
Rooting through the earth, grunting, furrowing
And foraging with his black snout, head down,
And a tail like a question, he crowned himself
The monarch of swinedom. *Le roi cochon.*

DESSALINES (*Stepping back.*)
Waiter . . .

CHRISTOPHE

Yes.

DESSALINES

Remember when I met you at L'Auberge de la Couronne?

CHRISTOPHE

Yes.

DESSALINES

When I had chains around my foot? Look there.
You can still see it. You remember all that?
Good. Then remember who you are talking to.

(CHRISTOPHE *picks up* DESSALINES*'s coat.*)

CHRISTOPHE

I know the work you were doing in there, and why
You have your coat flung down in the dirt. Here,
Wear it. You're supposed to be my Emperor, even

At six in the morning. This medal here, Toussaint
Gave you at D'Ennery. I stopped fighting to watch you,
Crouched at a gallop, your course fixed like a panther,
A black scream for your banner, you were then
The sword and reason of the war, left and right
You cutlassed legions of dragoons like sugar,
And wheeled round again like a tiger spinning
On its heel, till all the lances of the French legions
Were piled level as canes and there was nothing standing
Between your fury and the setting sun's.
And so it went, from Cap to Artibonite,
Across the ridges, the soldiers saw your body
Half-welded to its horse, like a black centaur,
And whispered, "This is an African, magical, singing
Sabres whistle through him and he joins his halves.
He slaps off bullets like mosquitoes, what
Chembois, what amulets preserve him?"
And I wondered myself, I lost myself
In utter and unutterable admiration
Like a man wandering through a forest
Whose compass is the moon, and when the moon went,
I took even a deeper pride in blackness,
In the night's skin; for us, you were the night,
The constellations were your medals,
The clouds, your plumes, you were a forest
Where our ancestral spirits lived, you were,
Jean Jacques. Then, you had majesty.
When you had nothing on your back
Which was already velvet, like a panther's,

Then you had grace, but what you are today
Turns the same eyes that watered with admiration
Away from you, makes us move from your shadow
As if it were a curse; you betray yourself,
One action noble, then the next one common,
One moment this, then the next moment that.
If you find peace has less purpose than war,
Then make a war inside you, fight with yourself,
And then I'd crown you myself, but all your actions
Endanger the republic, or what was once
A republic, before you made yourself a king.
Jean Jacques, the greatest king, the absolute monarch,
Is the man who knows his work has earned a crown
But who refuses it, or crowns the one who offers
It instead. You should give back the crown
To the republic, dissolve the monarchy,
Dissolve yourself, and then you'll know yourself.
And I'm saying what everyone around you feels
But is too scared to tell you.

(DESSALINES *weeps*.)

Tears may be good for us. When a king cries,
There's hope. That means he's still human.

DESSALINES

I think you said enough, yes.

CHRISTOPHE

       I said enough. Yes.
But I haven't written enough. Watch what I write.

(*He finds a stick.*)

DESSALINES

You know damn well I can't read. What is that?

(CHRISTOPHE *writes in the dirt with the stick.*)

CHRISTOPHE

Toussaint L'Ouverture. Jean Jacques Dessalines.
This one there is your name. No, this one here.
It is written in the Haitian earth forever.
Even if I scrape it out with my foot, like this.
(*He rubs out the names with his boot.*)

DESSALINES

Where's your name? Why you don't put it there?
So, you can write now. Me, I just use my stamp.
I am not a stick. I don't break. Where's the man
Who refused to work? Bring him here in front me
And you'll see who break. They have to plant,
They have to grow, they have to obey.
To make example, give him fifty lashes,
And since he won't listen, cut off his ear.

CHRISTOPHE

Not me. Not me again.

DESSALINES

Not you?

CHRISTOPHE

Not me, Jacko.

(*Silence.*)

DESSALINES

All right. Then me. Is I who do everything anyway.
I who begin, and I who end. You come in, you join
When everything was going good. I am the beginning,
And I am the end. Haiti is me. *Ous tendre?* This!
(*He stamps his foot.*)
Is. Me. I will send you his two ears.
(*He exits.*)

CHRISTOPHE

Jacques!

(*Two* LABOURERS, *barefooted, in dirty clothes, enter,
then wait.*)

FIRST LABOURER

*Monsieur Le Ministre, 'ous tais v'iler voir nous. Ous dit nous
espérer.*

CHRISTOPHE

'Jourd'hui.

(FIRST LABOURER *puts on a boar's head.*)

SECOND LABOURER

Eh bien, 'jourd'hui. If today is the day, today is the day.

CHRISTOPHE

The boar will find him, as he found the boar.
On the same beach. Do what you have to do.

(*Fade-out.*)

Scene 16

Belle Maison. 1820. A room. YETTE *rises out of bed and goes to a chest of drawers, one of which she pulls out carefully, so as not to wake* POMPEY. *She eases the drawer out, without looking down, watching her face in the dressing-table mirror steadily. Her hair is greying. She brings up an object from the bottom of the drawer. It is an effigy of* CHRISTOPHE, *doll-size, in coronation robes and with a little crown. The doll wears a crown, a figured golden robe, red coat, the Star of David on its tiny breast, its right cloth hand gripping a straw sceptre, its fat cloth legs splayed apart.*
YETTE *places a crucifix next to the doll king. She dips the pin in the paste. She heats and turns the long, sharp pin slowly in the flame. She rests the doll at an angle. She plucks a hair from her head sharply and lights a dressing-table candle. She burns the hair and draws it across the face of the black doll king. Fade-out.*

Scene 17

CHRISTOPHE's *palace. Night. Dressed exactly like the doll
but without a crown,* CHRISTOPHE *limps across the floor,
past the high arches to his throne, and sits there, squirming in
agony at the stabbing pain in his legs. Fade-out.*

Scene 18

*Belle Maison. For every stab of the heated pin into the doll's
leg,* CHRISTOPHE *wrenches and twists in agony.*
YETTE *keeps stabbing.*

YETTE
No more kings. No more kings. No more kings.

(*A* MAN *climbs over a rail, peeps at* YETTE *through
the window. She feels him watching her and turns. He
scurries away.*)

CHRISTOPHE
My crown! Bring me my crown! My crown!

(*Fade-out.*)

Scene 19

Interior. The palace. Morning. CHRISTOPHE *in his red coat
with its star, his leg propped on a stool. Behind him*

SOLDIERS. *On the floor is a huge scale model of the citadel at Sans Souci.* POMPEY *and* YETTE *enter.*

CHRISTOPHE

From the Hotel Couronne to this. I was a waiter.
A waiter. And this was a good leg.
Tell them again what she did to this waiter.
Say it, man.

SOLDIER

She prayed for victory for General Rigaud,
The enemy of our Emperor Henri Christophe.

CHRISTOPHE

Didn't you remember I was your King?
Perhaps you cannot believe in a black king!
You prayed for this mulatto. But of course.
You and he are the same people.
Did you see victory for Pétion? Eh?
For you and all the mulattos, eh? Mulatresse?

POMPEY

I will speak for her, with your permission.

CHRISTOPHE

She has a tongue. I know she has a tongue.
I knew her when she was the army's yellow whore.
(*Pause.*)

They say, these people,

You made *chienbois* against me. Is that true?

They say you prayed against me. Is that true?

(YETTE *nods.*)

Maybe she just like playing with dolls. Like children.

You all have children?

POMPEY

No.

CHRISTOPHE

Is she barren?

In Le Cap, in the big fire, I lost a child.

The soil can be dry. In your part of the country.

But never barren. You had a good crop this year?

(POMPEY *shrugs.*)

Do you see that thing there in front of you?

It is not the castle of a doll, men like you

Are building it now, on the ridge of Cap Haitien.

An army can march on the walls. If I tell that army

To march straight off into the precipice, they would

Obey me, to prove their obedience, as General Moise

Obeyed his uncle. It will be, after I choose to die,

One of the wonders of the world. When men like you

Are tired, they will look up into the clouds

And see it, and take strength; the clouds themselves

Will have to look up to see it. Does she think

Little pins in my legs will stop it?

Ask her. Why is she silent? Make her speak.

POMPEY

She is silent as the earth self silent, sir. Pardon me, yes, Your
Majesty. But I have seen so many kings, me and my woman
here, that we have to be afraid. One King say to us he is the
sun, and we niggers answer yes, and we was his shadows,
and the sun set, the King dead, and it was night again until
the next King come, and we again was shadows. It wasn't for
a king all this begin? I mean to say the King they kill in
France? Was not for that King, the sixteenth sun that rise
and the last King to set in France, that we came free? It had
no talk of king, then, Your Majesty. It was only poor people,
it was slaves, and those who work and die as if they was
white niggers under the sixteen kings of France, every one
a sunrise, every one a sunset, that Haiti live so long in a
long night. It had one talk then, I remember, under the
old coachman, and that talk was not who was king but
who would make each man a man, each man a king
himself; but all that change. We see them turn and climb
and burn and fall down like stars that tired, and cut my
hand, my head, my tongue out if you want, Your Majesty,
but my life is one long night. My country and your
kingdom, Majesty. One long, long night. Is kings who do
us that.

CHRISTOPHE

You work in dreams. Listen, last night, alone,
I had a terror of a dream. I saw the coachman
Drawing his country behind him like a black hearse
On a long, long road where stars were placed like candles,

And in the forest, on both sides, were little people
Born with their feet reversed, those mouse-eared elves
The boloms, and the black coach went on,
On the road to Guinea, it went along the road
On the sea, and the sea was silver, when it reached
The other side, they were all standing there,
Boukmann, and Biassou, and Moise, who shot himself
For discipline and example, and then the coachman
Came down and stroked the horses, then the coach,
And all the transparent shadows turned hard
Or changed into a forest, then the old coachman
Stood there between me, and something white was falling,
First I thought it was feathers, then it was snow.
If you have powers to see, tell 'em what it mean.

(YETTE *silent.*)

The woman must be punished. Executed. Hang her.
The man is free.

POMPEY

Free? When I was ever free?

Under you all?

CHRISTOPHE

You want to die with her?

(*He turns away.*)

POMPEY

For me not to die with her, Christophe,
Is the worse punishment that you could give me.

(YETTE *coughs.*)

YETTE

I have one thing to say. That will be all.
I never know I would ever find something stronger
Than you, *Ti-moune*. Stronger even than us.
Stronger and older than the love you teach me.
To love the earth. This. Here. The Haitian earth.
> (*She stamps her foot.*)
I am ready when you ready. *Au voir, Ti-moune.*

CHRISTOPHE

Come on, one of you. Help me into bed.
> (*He exits.*)

YETTE (*To the* SOLDIER)
Espérez. He love his country more than all of you!
He is the sweat and salt of the earth, this man.
And I prouder of him than if he was a king.
> (*She shouts.*)
Chantez chanson nous, Ti-moune, chantez,
Et prends courage. Chantez-lui fort, Pompey.
Don't beg them, Pompey. Don't beg, you not a slave!
> (*The* CHORUS *enters, as before.* YETTE *sings.*)
Haiti, Haiti, I shall love you.
I shall join the Haitian earth.
Suns shall set and rise above you,
Sunset death and sunrise birth.
> (*She climbs out of sight.*)

POMPEY, CHORUS, PEASANTS

They cannot take our faith from us,
We, who suffered many things,
All the soldiers, guns, and drummers,
All the emperors and kings.

(*A single drumbeat.* POMPEY *reenters, carrying* YETTE*'s*
body wrapped in a shroud. He shows her face.)

POMPEY

I have folded you up, the banner of my life.
Ah, Yette, *chérie,* I took your body down
To give enterrement in the Haitian earth.
You will turn into grass in a high wind,
You will have no regiments but the waving canes,
You will be a country woman with a basket
Walking down a red road in the high mountains.
(*He begins to dig the grave with a pitchfork, digging harder*
and harder. Fade-out.)